# 2006

## THE BEST 10-MINUTE PLAYS
## FOR THREE OR MORE ACTORS

# Smith and Kraus'
## Short Plays and 10-Minute Plays Collections

Christopher Durang Vol. I: 27 Short Plays

Frank D. Gilroy Vol. II: 15 One-Act Plays

Israel Horovitz Vol. I: 16 Short Plays

Romulus Linney 17 Short Plays

Terrence McNally Vol. I: 15 Short Plays

Lanford Wilson: 21 Short Plays

Act One Festival 1995: The Complete One-Act Plays

Act One Festival 1994: The Complete One-Act Plays

EST Marathon 1999: The Complete One-Act Plays

EST Marathon 1998: The Complete One-Act Plays

EST Marathon 1997: The Complete One-Act Plays

EST Marathon 1996: The Complete One-Act Plays

EST Marathon 1995: The Complete One-Act Plays

EST Marathon 1994: The Complete One-Act Plays

HB Playwrights Short Play Festival

    2003 The Subway Plays

    2002 The Beach Plays

    2001 The Hospital Plays

    2000 The Funeral Plays

    1999 The Airport Plays

    1998 The Museum Plays

    1997 The Motel Plays

Twenty One-Acts from 20 Years at the Humana Festival 1975–1995

The Women's Project and Productions Rowing to America and Sixteen Other Short Plays

8 TENS @ 8 Festival: 30 10-Minute Plays from the Santa Cruz Festivals I–VI

30 Ten-Minute Plays from the Actors Theatre of Louisville for 2 Actors

30 Ten-Minute Plays from the Actors Theatre of Louisville for 3 Actors

30 Ten-Minute Plays from the Actors Theatre of Louisville for 4, 5, and 6 Actors

2004: The Best 10-Minute Plays for Two Actors

2004: The Best 10-Minute Plays for Three or More Actors

2005: The Best 10-Minute Plays for Two Actors

2005: The Best 10-Minute Plays for Three or More Actors

# *2006*
# THE BEST 10-MINUTE PLAYS FOR THREE OR MORE ACTORS

Edited by D. L. Lepidus

CONTEMPORARY PLAYWRIGHT SERIES

A Smith and Kraus Book
Hanover, New Hampshire

Published by Smith and Kraus, Inc.
177 Lyme Road, Hanover, NH 03755
www.SmithandKraus.com
(888) 282-2881

First Edition: December 2007
10 9 8 7 6 5 4 3 2 1

Manufactured in the United States of America
Cover and Text Design by Julia Hill Gignoux, Freedom Hill Design
Cover photo by Harlan Taylor: Jay Russell, Mark Mineart, and Melinda Wade in
Jane Martin's *Listeners,* produced at the 2006 Humana Festival of New American Plays,
Actor's Theatre of Louisville.

ISBN-13 978-1-57525-564-4
ISSN 1550-6754
Library of Congress Control Number: 2007937064

# Contents

# Introduction

The ten-minute play as an accepted dramatic form is a fairly recent development. Some would say that its popularity is a result of our diminished
attention spans, which may be partially true; but here's how the genre came
to be.

For several years, Actors Theatre of Louisville, under the leadership of
Jon Jory, commissioned playwrights to write plays of short duration for performance by its apprentice company. This was a way for the theater to do
something to help playwrights, but also it was a way to develop relationships
with them, many of which bore fruit over the years as these writers went on
to have full-length plays staged in Actors Theater's famed Humana Festival.

Over the years, Actors Theatre built up quite a library of these short
plays, all of them in manuscript. An editor for the play publisher Samuel
French got the idea that maybe other theaters, actors, and students might be
interested in these plays if they were made available to them. He managed to
swing a deal for French to publish an anthology of Actors Theatre's best short
plays, which they were now calling "ten-minute plays." This anthology was so
successful that French has now published six such volumes, and most of the
other publishers have followed suit, including Smith and Kraus, as its annual
ten-minute plays anthologies will attest. Bills of ten-minute plays are now
produced regularly — all over the world.

There are some who feel that the ten-minute play ought to be an oppor-
tunity for playwrights to experiment — with language, with form, with character, with subject matter. "The best" ten-minute plays are therefore the ones
that depart the most from conventional drama. For the purposes of this series,
here is how I define "best": that which is most useful to people who will buy
this book and produce these plays. Some actors and directors prefer straight-
forward realism; whereas others go for more abstract, experimental plays. I
don't carry a torch for any one style, so I have tried to include in this book
examples of realism and, shall we say, "non-realism." I hope you will find
herein more than one play that rings your bell. They all rang mine.

Should you find a play (or plays) in this book that you want to produce, you will find information in the back on who to contact for performance rights.

*D. L. Lepidus*
*Brooklyn, N.Y.*

# PLAYS FOR
# THREE ACTORS

# The Last Woman on Earth

## A Ten-Minute Countdown

LIZ DUFFY ADAMS

CHARACTERS
> EARTHLING: woman, looks anywhere from late twenties to early thirties
>
> CAPTAIN: woman, same age range; an authoritative, martial presence. She's wearing some kind of uniform, probably red.
>
> LUNATIC: younger man, wearing only something like a Mylar kilt and boots, and flimsy-looking silvery wings.

SETTING
> Earth, 2509 AD

PRODUCTION NOTES
> The cast must be multiethnic. The future is not white. This is a count-down, meant to be played urgently — almost no pauses.

· · ·

EARTHLING: *(Shouting over the audience's heads:)* Take off! Take off! I'm going down with the ship! Take yourself off with your infernal future tense, leave me to my eternal peace, ship off, shove off, piss off and kiss off and get off my stinking rock, end!
> *(Ends brain-mail with short sharp cock of head.)*
> *(To audience:)* O my beloved ghost sheep. Don't think I would ever leave you. We've only ten minutes but in that time no one will ever have loved you as I will. Soon in some sense we'll be together for all eternity, or we won't, we won't. Either way, an end to all suspense, once and for all, all, all. I'm hoping for oblivion myself, but that's my own damned fault. Never did know when to leave a party.
> *(Captain strides in, followed by Lunatic who runs in a full circle around Earthling, ending near the Captain, staring at Earthling.)*

CAPTAIN: Listen up, we've got — what?

LUNATIC: *(Eyes on Earthling:)* Nine minutes thirty, Captain my Captain.

CAPTAIN: Nine minutes thirty and down-counting, no time for philosophy, my orders are clear, get on the ship.

EARTHLING: And they say charm is a lost art.

CAPTAIN: Did I not say no time? No time! Everyone else has evacuated. In — what?

LUNATIC: Nine minutes twenty, Captain my Captain.

CAPTAIN: — this rock will be a dead world, complete annihilation, there will be no here here, end of the world time, you're the last one left, my orders are clear, it's eviction time, right? Get on the Goddamned ship.

EARTHLING: Gosh, this is repetitive. Do you know who I am?

LUNATIC: *(On a breath:)* Yeah.

CAPTAIN: You're the oldest, yes, you're the Ancient Earthling, the first to live forever, or would be, the walking millennium, the Venerable Bubula, so Goddamned what, we gotta go, in — what?

LUNATIC: Nine minutes mark, Captain my Captain.

EARTHLING: In eight minutes or less you'll leave without me. In the meantime be civil or fuck off. I don't care to spend the rest of my life arguing.

CAPTAIN: *(To Lunatic:)* Go back. Tell them — *(Turns him upstage and murmurs in his ear.)*

EARTHLING: *(To audience:)* O my darling dead ones, don't think I've forgotten you. In the name of everything most earthly and secular-sacred, of dirt and blood and oxygen, I won't forsake you, I won't be saved, we'll go down with the ship together. Not long now. Gosh, you're beautiful. I'm not kidding, you really are. I can see your little hearts pulsing away, right through your sweet spectral bodies. Boom, boom, boom, the rhythm of oblivion. Not long now.

CAPTAIN: *(To Lunatic, out loud:)* Go on.

LUNATIC: Ay-yi-yi, Captain, my Captain.

*(He runs around in a lurching circle as if trying to take off.)*

CAPTAIN: Just walk! Gravity!

*(Lunatic stops, embarrassed, then runs out.)*

EARTHLING: Lunatic?

CAPTAIN: Born on the Moon. First time on the Original World.

EARTHLING: What level?

CAPTAIN: What he looks like, first level. No treatments.

EARTHLING: So young. Your boy?

CAPTAIN: My adjunct.

EARTHLING: I meant, you fucking him?

CAPTAIN: What's that, earthiness? *(Cocks head to initiate brain-mail:)* TIME. GOT IT. END. *(To Earthling:)* Eight minutes ten.

EARTHLING: It's going to be an unutterably tedious eight minutes ten if you don't shut up about the fucking time.

CAPTAIN: Just trying to inject a note of urgency.

EARTHLING: It's a clumsy device. We all know how long we've got. Not even long enough for a dying screw. We could manage a nice sloppy kiss.

How about it? I know we've just met but as we know, the clock's ticking . . . Not if I were the last woman on Earth, huh?

CAPTAIN: I've got my orders.

EARTHLING: You're from what, Mars?

CAPTAIN: I'm a Martian, yes. Born and bred red. Why do you want to stay? Suicidal?

EARTHLING: You say it like it's a bad thing. Such a gentle, sibilant word. Soo-i-sssi-De. Ooh, that got you.

CAPTAIN: It's inhuman, immoral, unpatriotic, the worst kind of species disloyalty, number one on the list of prohibited acts, selfish, wicked, and vile. Your own planetary CEO specifically denounced it following the last radical purge.

EARTHLING: Where's our Chief now, anyway, half-way to the Outer Rim? "The sky is falling!"

CAPTAIN: She's leading the evacuation, yes.

EARTHLING: As a coward leads the running away.

CAPTAIN: Traitor.

EARTHLING: Me-ow.

*(Lunatic runs back in.)*

Hey, loonie, you back?

*(Lunatic flashes Earthling a look, runs around in circle, reports back to Captain.)*

LUNATIC: Captain my Captain, ship's lawyers say we can't take her by force —

CAPTAIN: Damn it!

*(Pulls him upstage so Earthling can't hear.)*

EARTHLING: *(To audience:)* I'm sorry, darling departed, I'm so sorry you saw me flirting with that boy. Believe me, he means nothing to me. He's only flesh and blood and appalling youth, and yes, old habits, blood rises, lust leaps, but oh, my dears, my heart is yours. You'll take me in, won't you, you'll wrap me in your night's embrace, we'll sleep together for eternity or so, won't we? So soon, when these fripperies leave and the sky cracks and out comes the yolk of time . . . all right, that didn't quite make sense, the curse of apocalyptic poetry. You'll forgive me, yes, because I do love you?

CAPTAIN: *(Coming back down:)* All right, look, we've got, what —

LUNATIC: Six minutes twenty, Captain my —

EARTHLING: How old are you, Captain?

CAPTAIN: Second level. Eighty-seven.

EARTHLING: I'm 500 or so. You do stop counting. I could look it up.

LUNATIC: *(On a breath:)* Five hundred and twelve.

EARTHLING: Really? The last fifty or so have been such a blur. Faster and faster.

CAPTAIN: Your point being?

EARTHLING: Blunted, I'm afraid.

CAPTAIN: Look —

EARTHLING: I have looked, dear Captain, and I have seen. I have heard, I have smelt and I have tasted and I have touched. Five hundred and twelve years of mornings — how's your math, Lunar boy?

LUNATIC: One hundred and eighty-six thousand, eight hundred and eighty —

EARTHLING: Wakings up alone or curling into the sleepy warmth, and — how many?

LUNATIC: One hundred eighty-six thousand eight hundred eighty —

EARTHLING: First hot liquid mouthfuls of coffee, and — what was it?

LUNATIC: *(Getting into a rhythm:)* One-eight-six-eight-eighty —

EARTHLING: Baths and — what you say?

LUNATIC: One-eight-six-eight-eighty —

EARTHLING: Plans and — sing it little brother!

LUNATIC: One-eight-six-eight-eighty —

EARTHLING: Fiddling with keys or card-locks or retinal scans and that's only the mornings!

CAPTAIN: You're tired? Is that all it is, you're just tired?

EARTHLING: Fuck yes, I'm tired, I'm fucking whacked but that's not it, that's not my POINT, it's memories, Christ's sake, I'm FULL. Every word you say is lodging itself into a FULL HOUSE. Not a question of good memories, bad memories, acres and acres of ordinary memories, I'm full, it's too much, I don't want any more. From the moment my dad woke me up one midnight and said, look, honey, it's the new millennium, you'll always remember this. And now he's been dead four hundred and forty years and I'm a walking graveyard of memory. I'm the only living human to remember graveyards, or automobiles or cassette players or who the Beatles were. I remember phone numbers and street addresses when there are no longer phones or streets. I remember a swaybacked horse in a muddy field, a flock of tiny black birds over a marsh, burning cold feet in ice skates as twilight fell. I remember the crash of two thousand and one, the Accidental Armageddon of '23, the great biodiversity crisis of the mid-twenty-first. I can still smell the acrid smoke of the fall of New York. I have a scar on my back from the mutant riots of twenty-three-thirty and a lingering glow in my heart from the first wave of the Re-enlightenment. I remember the great gleaming space-liners taking off full of emigrants when the New Colonial Period began, the piercing cries of seagulls after the roar of engines died away and the emptiness of the streets afterwards. And I remember everyone I ever fucked and every one I loved, I remember endless snatches of then crucially bitter or joyful conversations, I remember embarrassing moments from centuries ago — natch — I know the lyrics of a billion idiot pop songs, the plots of millions of novels and movies and sense-o-sagas, I know a thousand-year-old children's game. Ashes, ashes, but I don't fall down. *(To Lunatic:)* How long?

LUNATIC: Three minutes five, Earthling my Earthling.

EARTHLING: The two of you better run along.

CAPTAIN: When you come with us.

EARTHLING: Oh, come on! This is beyond the call of duty. What on Earth — well, you know what I mean — What's it to you?

CAPTAIN: Duty is enough.

EARTHLING: To a Martian maybe. Don't mean jack to a Dirtbag.

CAPTAIN: All right. Well. Fact is. You're my ancestor. You're my direct ancestor.

EARTHLING: I thought Martians frowned on genealogy, especially pre-colonial.

CAPTAIN: They do. I do. A lot of damned nonsense really. Well. That's what I thought. Then I got plugged in to a — this is off the record.

EARTHLING: It'll be incinerated soon with all the rest of my memories.

CAPTAIN: I got plugged in to a piece of contraband genealogical bio-ware. I got hooked. I'm clean now. But I know what I know.

EARTHLING: Oh, anyway, so what? So fucking what? I have as many descendants as a month-old cockroach, what's it add up to?

CAPTAIN: You are needed. We need you. We are losing the home world. No big deal really, not a species survival issue, we have terreformed plenty of planets, nicer planets, fresher, better-organized. Most people will watch it on the news, enjoy a moment of info-tain-pseudo-trag. And move on. But something will be lost, and some of us will know it. You're a symbol to the species. A beacon of continuity and hope. A link with the past as we head into the unknown future.

EARTHLING: And a monster of selfishness, because utterly unmoved. No sale, Captain. I can be all that when I'm dead. Sorry, game over, go on, go.

CAPTAIN: *(Slight pause, then snaps head for brain-mail:)* WE'RE COMING UP. IMMEDIATE TAKE OFF. STAND BY. END.

*(Looks at Earthling, too pissed-off to say good-bye, begins to stride off.)*

EARTHLING: Captain.

*(She stops.)*

Think of me in 400 years.

*(Slight pause. Captain exits. Lunatic starts to follow, then comes back to Earthling.)*

LUNATIC: *(Softly:)* Two minutes three.

EARTHLING: Sweet lunatic. You'd better fly away.

LUNATIC: I did you in school.

EARTHLING: You, you what?

LUNATIC: I got my degree in you. A B.A.E. Bachelor of Ancient Earthling. Please come.

EARTHLING: Would you help me to forget?

LUNATIC: I would.

EARTHLING: Show me.

*(Lunatic kisses her.)*

For this relief much thanks, gentle Lunatic.

LUNATIC: Will you come?

EARTHLING: You tempt me. But have mercy and let me go.

*(Lunatic regards her.)*

LUNATIC: I'll remember you.

*(Lunatic exits.)*

EARTHLING: *(To audience:)* Did you think I was going to say yes? I admit, I was tempted. But you didn't really want me to go with him, did you? Did you? Clap if you believe in fairies, and I'll run after him. O, darling ghost sheep, alone at last. But you don't know why I call you ghost sheep, do you? We've just time for one brief story. Once upon a time, nearly five hundred years ago, I was walking near a forest. I came upon a sad farmer in a feed-store cap, who had lost two sheep days before. I told him I'd keep my eye out, and he said sadly, "It don't matter. You can't catch sheep." Well, I walked through the forest, and soon forgot about the farmer. Until one moment, I looked up, and there ahead on the trail stood two sheep, white fleece glowing ghost-like in the dim leafy light. One had a wide white face, and one had a thin black face, and they looked at me beseechingly, I thought, trembling a little, weary and lost. O sheep, I murmured. Come to me and I'll lead you to safety. But with my first step toward them, they lost faith, they panicked, they fled away into the woods, they wouldn't be caught. And I was forced to leave them there, and soon, I'm afraid, they must have become ghost sheep indeed. And now that I've told you, I realize I got it wrong. You're my dear ghosts. But I'm your lost sheep. Put your arms around my woolly neck and lead me home. Five, four, three, two — *(The world ends.)*

END OF PLAY

# Stop the Lawns

P. SETH BAUER

*For my brother Mark*

*Stop the Lawns* was originally commissioned by The DrillingCompany (artistic director Hamilton Clancy) and presented at 78th Street Theatre Lab on December 3, 2005. It was directed by Gabriele Forster, with sets by Rebecca Lord, lighting by Miriam Nilofa Crowe, and stage management by Billie Davis with the following cast: Zan — Tobias Segal; Tunge — Alessandro Colla; Noah — Michael Schreiber.

CHARACTERS
    ZAN
    TUNGE
    NOAH

SETTING
    A basement

•  •  •

*Zan, Tunge, and Noah lay around in some basement.*

ZAN: Mowing lawns. We're like little ants, moving lawns back and forth across town. In little rows.

TUNGE: And it just all fucking grows back.

ZAN: Exactly. Mowed lawns. The lawns are always growing. As soon as I finish fucking mowing. Man. You can like even see them growing back real slow but they're there just coming back to get you. Mowing lawns is an endless thing.

TUNGE: Man that's fucking awesome. Zan's all like Japanese. An endless thing!

ZAN: It's true, they'll never stop those lawns.

ZAN AND TUNGE: They keep growing and growing and growing.

TUNGE: Someone should put an end to that shit.

ZAN: That's right. He's right! Someone must take a stand against those lawns, really put it to them.

TUNGE: Chemical warfare. Like Weedwackers and shit.

*(Zan gets up to pace and work it out.)*

ZAN: We've got to stop the lawns man. Cuz I'm mowing 'em now. Right, I'm one of those little ants making those long straight rows right now, I'm part of the problem, the system. And I know in my gut — I'll always be mowing that lawn man. It's a horrifying reality.

TUNGE: And shitting.

ZAN: What?

TUNGE: You'll always be like — shitting and what not. You know pissing and shitting.

ZAN: Exactly. Why do I want to do that with my life?

TUNGE: You need a higher purpose dude.

ZAN: Man Tunge is on. You're like connected yo. He's all plugged in, checking it all out, watching, taking notes, taking down the details. He's a witness T. He's eyeing the scene like a magazine.

NOAH: Fuck off.

*(Zan and Tunge laugh.)*

TUNGE: Dude you got to plant that shit.

ZAN: Jerk off over there. We don't mind.

TUNGE: No I don't mind.

ZAN: No seriously Noah. Serious. I know you're feeling lonely and you've got all this extra juice. So if, seriously, if you need someplace to put it. Just go upstairs and fuck my dog.

*(Tunge flips out.)*

ZAN: No seriously she's nice, you've always liked her.

TUNGE: He's been watching her hind quarters.

ZAN: She's a good dog, she won't mind.

TUNGE: She'll probably sleep through it.

NOAH: Just like your mother.

ZAN: Yeah just like Mom yo.

*(Casually rapping)*

Your mother, your mother, your sister, your brother.

NOAH: Fuck you.

ZAN: I'd do it but you're not family so —

TUNGE: Dude so what'd she say?

NOAH: Who?

TUNGE: Becky yo. Seriously was she all like, "Let's be friends" or —

ZAN: "I don't want it to get in the way of our friendship" —

TUNGE: "I think of you as a friend" —

ZAN: "As a friend" —

TUNGE: "with a small dick."

NOAH: My dick is small. My dick is crooked. It goes to the right and leans up at the end. So what does it fucking matter? So fuck you and fuck you.

*(He points a gun at them both.)*

ZAN: Whoa whoa whoa check that out. Check out Clint Eastwood dude.

TUNGE: Where'd you get that yo?

NOAH: Off a guy in a place in a store on a street.

TUNGE: How much?

NOAH: Four lawns and a coke.

TUNGE: Seriously. Man we should get guns.

ZAN: Yeah that way we'll get ahead in life.

TUNGE: I'm serious check this out. Yo point that at him.

ZAN: Fuck you.

TUNGE: No see look at Noah. He's all like — he looks different now yo.

ZAN: He looks insane.

NOAH: Really.

TUNGE: Oh man you know what we should do.

ZAN: Kill somebody.

TUNGE: We should fucking kill somebody.

ZAN: That's a good idea. Then we wouldn't be so bored.

TUNGE: Least we wouldn't have to mow anymore lawns.

ZAN: Why not?

TUNGE: Cuz we'd be in prison dude. Or on the run, Mexico. Or dead. Those are the options. And none of them include lawns.

ZAN: Tunge. Thinking outside the box. Like the birds in the sky, looking down at the ants the ground. Is Tunge.

TUNGE: The Master.

NOAH: Wait you guys want to kill somebody instead of mowing lawns.

ZAN: Don't you?

NOAH: I don't know.

ZAN: Dude why'd you pick that up?

NOAH: I don't know. Kill myself I guess.

ZAN: Dude don't kill yourself. Kill him.

TUNGE: What?

ZAN: I said for him to kill you.

TUNGE: Yeah kill me.

NOAH: Really?

TUNGE: Yeah.

NOAH: You're sure.

TUNGE: Totally.

NOAH: Alright.

    *(Noah shoots Tunge.)*

ZAN: Oh my God. You fuckin' mad man.

NOAH: He said to do it.

ZAN: You are fucking out there dude.

NOAH: Is he dead?

ZAN: I don't know. He is shot though.

NOAH: Man. That feels so . . .

ZAN: Shit we gotta do something.

NOAH: No wait.

ZAN: Get him to the hospital, is your car outside?

NOAH: So amazing . . .

ZAN: Dude you got to chill. Help me get him up the stairs. Oh man Jesus.

NOAH: Feels so relaxing. I shoulda done this a long time ago.

ZAN: Tunge you hear me? You're gonna be cool — you look real good.

*(Zan holds up Tunge who is clearly seriously wounded, blood everywhere.)*

TUNGE: You totally shot me dude.

NOAH: I know. Isn't that fucked up?

TUNGE: No man, I'm like a banner headline, "The Tunge has been shot."

NOAH: And I'm like a murderer.

TUNGE: You are dude.

NOAH: I'm like a Noah, the Anti-Noah killing all the animals before they get off the ark. It's so great . . . this is so much better than dating or sex and what not. Going to college and all that bullshit.

ZAN: All those lawns.

NOAH: All those motherfucking lawns.

ZAN: This is like a crime scene. My basement is like *The Silence of the Lambs.* I mean they'll come down here and see like my mom's dishware and like my old bicycle and that'll be in pictures in the crime lab.

TUNGE: Am I dying?

ZAN: I don't know dude.

TUNGE: Well what color's my blood?

ZAN: It looks like blood right.

TUNGE: Darker or light.

NOAH: It's coming out dark now.

TUNGE: Cool. Won't be long now!

ZAN: For real?

NOAH: Yeah he's draining. Are you psyched?

TUNGE: Oh man yeah, I get to fast-forward all that and check that shit out.

ZAN: Are you scared?

TUNGE: No it's a rush.

ZAN: No I mean about the other side.

TUNGE: No man, it's like skydiving toward oblivion yo. I'll figure it out when I get there.

ZAN: We should get him to the hospital.

NOAH: He looks good there.

TUNGE: No hospital. If they saved me I'd just be like the kid who got shot and got better.

NOAH: Do you want us to call anybody?

TUNGE: No man. Let's just chill out here. Somebody light me up.

ZAN: Oh yeah dude. Totally.

*(They light up joints.)*

NOAH: So simple. I don't know why we never thought of this before.

ZAN: We just wait here?

NOAH: I guess.

ZAN: Tunge do you want a last meal or whatever, taste some pussy?

TUNGE: Is the dog down here?

*(They laugh.)*

ZAN: Seriously.

TUNGE: I'm good.

ZAN: So am I like an accomplice?

NOAH: Yeah, I think so.

ZAN: Wow. Cool.

NOAH: No more lawns man.

ZAN: No more lawns.

*(They sit and wait for death.)*

END OF PLAY

# Dining Outdoors

VINCENT DELANEY

CHARACTERS

NICOLE

JULIA

MIKE: a waiter

SETTING

A very nice restaurant

. . .

*A very nice restaurant, outdoors, a verandah with a view. Sound of birds, a waterfall. Nicole and Julia enter. Nicole is struggling with seven or eight shopping bags, Julia carries nothing.*

NICOLE: People are so rude. I have scratches, all over my arms. It's just a semi-annual sale, you'd think those women could behave themselves. Look at these marks! Those bitches are animals. It wasn't even a great sale. I think I'm depressed.

*(They sit.)*

NICOLE: It's a nice view. What do you think of the view?

JULIA: Could we sit inside?

NICOLE: We reserved the verandah.

*(Mike enters, friendly and peppy.)*

MIKE: Good evening ladies. My name is Mike. Can I tell you about our appetizers?

NICOLE: Why?

MIKE: Because . . . you . . . might like to try one?

NICOLE: Bring me a sweet and sour pina colada with a butternut twist, warm, not hot. My friend wants a hot rum vanilla toddy with chocolate shavings.

JULIA: Could I have water? Just water?

NICOLE: You don't want the hot toddy?

JULIA: Just water. Please.

MIKE: I could tell you about the appetizers.

*(An awkward silence. He goes.)*

NICOLE: I hate waiters. They are so dishonest. Did you buy any lingerie?

JULIA: It's so bright out here.

NICOLE: Bloomingdale's had a fur-lined sequined teddy. That is just obscene.

I got one in red, one in black. Maybe Jared's little worm will come out of hiding. How about you?

JULIA: Sure.

NICOLE: Did you see the suede boots at Nordstrom's? I had to fight a lipo candidate to get the last pair. I hope she dies during surgery.

JULIA: Yes.

NICOLE: Don't blame Nordstrom's. It's not the store's fault. Women should be able to control themselves at a sales event.

JULIA: Are those robins? That sound?

NICOLE: Probably. Birds, anyway. Or something small that chirps.

JULIA: I don't see them.

NICOLE: So. Did you get anything naughty?

JULIA: No.

NICOLE: Uh huh. I know how Justin is. You married a beast. Not like me, I married a garden hose. Let's go out to your Hummer, you can show me everything. No one can shop like you, Julia.

*(Mike returns.)*

MIKE: Here's your water. The pina colada will be right up. What do you think of our view?

NICOLE: I didn't know it was yours. Your personal view.

MIKE: Um. I suppose it's not my own, personal . . .

NICOLE: But you take credit for it. That's nice, Mike.

JULIA: Are those robins?

MIKE: Where?

JULIA: The sound. Are they robins?

MIKE: I never heard that before. I suppose they must be birds.

JULIA: Never?

MIKE: Maybe I never noticed them. Perhaps you'd like to hear about our dinner specials?

NICOLE: Why?

MIKE: Because . . . yes. Yes, I see.

*(An awkward silence. He goes. This time he remains in sight, listening to the birds.)*

NICOLE: Look at him. What a fake.

JULIA: He seemed very nice.

NICOLE: Exactly. Do you think he's actually nice? Or that he cares about you? Waiters are the phoniest profession. Most of them aren't even waiters at all. They're starving actors. Why are there never any real waiters? Is that fair? Would you let some starving actor fix your car? Do you want one of them operating on your thighs? Then why do we have to accept table service from them? For once I wish I could be served by an actual waiter.

JULIA: You think he's an actor?

NICOLE: Look at his face. There's something shrewish and driven about him. That's an actor.

JULIA: He hears us.

NICOLE: Good, he knows we can't be messed with. Oh my God. Look at that. By the railing. Red sweater. You see?

JULIA: The blonde?

NICOLE: Not her hair. Although that's also a disaster. Lower.

JULIA: Ooh.

NICOLE: They are so fake. They don't even move together. The left one goes up, the right one just hangs there.

JULIA: I feel bad for her.

NICOLE: Her surgeon must have been drunk. I'd sue.

JULIA: They aren't that far out of synch.

NICOLE: They're supposed to work as a team. There are no points for individuality.

JULIA: She hears. She's looking this way.

NICOLE: Let her look. My breasts are perfect.

JULIA: They really are.

NICOLE: So are yours, silly. Are you feeling all right? It's the sale, I know. I get so demoralized after a big sale. You work so hard, and somehow you end up buying absolutely nothing. Let's get smashed.

JULIA: I can't do that.

NICOLE: What's the matter?

JULIA: I have to stay ready.

NICOLE: Oh. What?

JULIA: We're so exposed here. So much open space.

NICOLE: Oh, honey. Did you go off Paxil? You can't just go off it, you know that. You'll get so depressed.

JULIA: Where did she go?

NICOLE: Who?

JULIA: The blonde woman. She was at the edge.

NICOLE: So? She left.

JULIA: She would have had to walk past us. She was at the edge. Oh my God. Oh my God!

NICOLE: She probably just —

JULIA: She fell. She's down there. We have to help her.

NICOLE: Something's the matter. Tell me. Justin's seeing someone else. Honey, that's OK, that just means he can still get erections. It's a positive thing. The more he wants other women, the more you can still profit.

*(Mike returns with a tray of appetizers.)*

JULIA: Did you see her? The blonde woman?

MIKE: The boob job?

JULIA: I think she jumped. Oh my God, I think she jumped.

NICOLE: Because we insulted her? Please.

JULIA: How far down is it?

MIKE: Pretty far. She probably just walked out. These are from us. Enjoy.

NICOLE: We didn't order those.

MIKE: With our compliments.

NICOLE: Why?

MIKE: No particular reason.

NICOLE: Is it a promotion?

MIKE: No.

NICOLE: A product sample?

MIKE: No.

NICOLE: You're promoting a credit card?

MIKE: They're on us. Just because.

NICOLE: You're going to charge us. You have to charge us something.

MIKE: They're free.

NICOLE: You can't just give food away. That's wrong.

MIKE: They're free!

*(An awkward silence. Mike can't take it any longer. He explodes.)*

MIKE: Our specials include a broiled Alaska salmon in a wild rice cream sauce, with asparagus tips and compote. Or the prime rib, served rare with a tangy spice medley and choice of potato. We also have a garlic baked tandoori chicken, served in a mini-kiln with basmati rice and chutney.

*(Mike takes a breath, relieved. He steps away.)*

JULIA: I didn't buy anything. Today. At the sale.

NICOLE: Nothing?

JULIA: Nothing.

NICOLE: We were there four hours. Everything's discounted 40 to 70 percent. How could you not buy anything? Oh my God. Did Justin lose his job?

JULIA: I sat in the food court. In a corner. I watched people eat. Hundreds of people. Making messes, eating, belching. Not aware. Not looking. Not alert.

NICOLE: You didn't buy anything? There's nothing in the Hummer? The Hummer is empty?

JULIA: I don't think she jumped. I think she was pulled over. Taken.

NICOLE: Oh for God's sake — wait here.

JULIA: Where are you going? No!

NICOLE: I'm going to look! I'm going to show you she's not down there!

*(Julia clutches her, terrified.)*

JULIA: No! Please! Don't go over there, Nicole. Stay with me. Please. Just stay here.

NICOLE: There's nothing wrong, silly. Here, eat, have a meat stick, or whatever it is.

*(Julia throws the food onto the floor.)*

JULIA: Get it away, get it away, don't touch it! Keep back from it!

*(A beat.)*

NICOLE: Are you having a bad day?

*(Mike returns with a drink, extremely cheerful.)*

MIKE: One sweet and sour pina colada with a hazelnut twist. This is one of my favorite drinks, actually. Sometimes when I'm off my shift I'll kick back and . . .

*(They're staring at him. An awkward silence.)*

MIKE: Is there anything else I can bring you right now?

NICOLE: You could bring me my drink.

MIKE: I'm sorry?

NICOLE: I didn't order this glass of urine, Mike.

MIKE: But you said —

NICOLE: I said butternut, Mike. I didn't order a hazelnut twist, Mike. If I'd wanted a hazelnut, I'd go to the Rain Forest Café with the trailer trash and their diaper-swaddled shit factories, Mike.

MIKE: I'm sorry, but I'm sure you said —

NICOLE: I hate hazelnut! I would never order hazelnut! I know what makes me retch, and the things that make me retch I don't order! Are you telling me I like to retch, Mike? I own three homes, Mike. They all have garages, although I don't drive. I have three Subzeros, even though I don't cook! I know how to order, Mike! It's what I do for a living! Knowing how to order is how we define civilization, Mike!

JULIA: I'm being hunted.

NICOLE: What?

JULIA: I killed something. Last night. With the Hummer. Iridescent eyes, golden. Shining up at me. I ran it over.

NICOLE: Something . . .

JULIA: Big. Like a lion. Bigger. Sinewy, strong, golden muscles. I startled it, it was feeding in the street. It froze, snarled, I don't know, I couldn't stop in time, I was distracted, I tried to swerve, I ran it over.

NICOLE: A cat? You hit a cat?

JULIA: I felt it die. Through the wheels.

*(Silence.)*

MIKE: Just because I wait tables, doesn't mean I don't deserve respect.

*(Mike goes off.)*

JULIA: It was a male. There was a mate, I didn't see her, but she must have seen me do it. I drove home, I was upset, I cried in the car. When I got out the front door was torn open. Like a cyclone. There was blood, the walls, everything was ripped. I think she took Justin. I think he's gone.

NICOLE: Justin.

JULIA: I thought I'd be safe in the mall, all the people. I tried to hide. Concentrate, stay focused. She was watching. Stalking me. She was there. She's out there now, over the edge, waiting for me. Down there.

NICOLE: Julia. You hit a cat.

JULIA: She knows I'm here. She's not going to let me leave. This is going to be the end.

NICOLE: There are no lions in the city!

JULIA: There are lots of them! Lots of them! We just don't see them.

NICOLE: All right. I'm going to call Justin on my cell. OK? You can talk with him. He's fine.

JULIA: He won't answer. She has him.

*(Nicole dials.)*

NICOLE: Excuse me, waiter? Waiter? What the hell was his — Mike? Mike, could you come back for a moment? Please? I'm sorry, the drink is great. Mike!

*(Silence.)*

NICOLE: He must have stormed out. That is so unprofessional.

*(A loud thump as something heavy falls offstage, where Mike went.)*

NICOLE: He's not answering.

JULIA: My poor husband.

NICOLE: He's probably in the subway, he'll pick up in a minute.

JULIA: And the blonde woman.

NICOLE: Waiter! Where is that waiter? I'll go check.

JULIA: Please. Nicole. Don't leave me.

NICOLE: We'll eat uptown. Somewhere urban, with a nice view of cement. How does that sound? Sound good?

JULIA: Listen.

*(Silence.)*

JULIA: The birds have stopped.

NICOLE: So?

JULIA: I think this is it. I think they know.

NICOLE: Stay here. I mean it. Don't move. I'll get the bill.

*(Nicole starts off.)*

JULIA: Nicole? I've always liked you. I really have.

*(Nicole doesn't answer. She goes off after Mike. A pause. A loud thump as something else goes down. Julia is alone.)*

JULIA: I would like to say. Just, that, I'm sorry. It's not an excuse, I don't expect — we've been bad. All of us. Toward you, all of you. Maybe, well, we deserve it. Maybe we do. You won't forgive me. I know that. But I'm still very sorry. We haven't been as good as we could be. Toward all of you. And we knew better.

*(She sips the pina colada. Takes a breath. Takes off her jacket, drapes it over the chair, slow and deliberate. Lays her purse down carefully. And walks off-stage.)*

*(A silence. A loud thump.)*

END OF PLAY

# Grave

SARAH GAVITT

Presented as part of the American Globe Theatre/Turnip
Theatre Company 15-Minute Play Festival, April 24, 2006.
Cast: Marci — Becky Kramer; Liesel — Nomi Tichman;
Robbie — Jonathan Medina. Directed by Sarah Gavitt.

CHARACTERS

    MARCY: nineteen

    LIESEL: her older sister

    ROBBIE: a carpenter

SETTING

    A backyard

• • •

## SCENE 1

*Night. A backyard. There is a gravestone. An egg hits the gravestone. Another egg. Another. Silence. A backyard light turns on.*

MARCY: *(Calls from out her window.)* Get away from my dad!
    *(Marcy enters from the back door of the house. She has some paper towels. She walks to the gravestone. She wipes at the egg.)*
    I'm sorry about that. I really am.
    *(Marcy looks skyward.)*
    Do you know who that was? Did you see his face?
    *(Blackout.)*

## SCENE 2

*Morning. Marcy sits on a chaise lounge.*

LIESEL: *(With a garbage bag.)* I called a guy to fix the fence. He'll be here at eleven.

MARCY: It won't make a difference.

LIESEL: These bags are so cheap. What is this, mayonnaise? God, I hope so.

MARCY: I'm gonna sleep out here tonight.

LIESEL: Do you think that's safe?

MARCY: I've got a camera this time.

LIESEL: This is so gross. I'm getting a brand-name next time.

MARCY: You don't even care.

LIESEL: Don't tell me what I think.

MARCY: I'm not talking about thinking I'm talking about feeling.

LIESEL: Look, he'll be here at eleven. He'll fix the fence. End of problem.
    *(Liesel exits. Marcy reads.)*

## SCENE 3

*Robbie is pounding a nail into two boards. He works in silence.*

ROBBIE: Good book?

MARCY: I guess.

ROBBIE: *(Reading the title.)* Greek Tragedies. Looks good. So . . . this is like, your dad?

MARCY: Yes.

ROBBIE: Hm. It ever creep you out?

MARCY: No.

ROBBIE: That's cool. Your sister said somebody's out to get him.

MARCY: There was a — I don't know.

ROBBIE: My mom wants to be cremated. She wants her ashes put in Lake Eerie. That's where her family vacationed all the time when she was a kid. So, this guy like broke in through the fence?

MARCY: The fence was already broken.

ROBBIE: Oh. How's that?

MARCY: It's been broken. For awhile.

ROBBIE: Think he'll try to get in again?

MARCY: Yes.

ROBBIE: You call the police?

MARCY: No.

ROBBIE: You should put up signs or something. Wanted posters. You got a description?

MARCY: Couldn't see.

ROBBIE: Huh. I guess that would kinda piss me off too.

## SCENE 4

MARCY: Nobody's beeswax.

Alright then, four months. One season ago.

The ground was gooey because of the rain. We could have dug it with our bare hands.

Our dog, Scarfey, is out here. Closer to the fence. We didn't mark the grave because we didn't want him to feel committed. That was my dad's idea.

We want him to return to the earth without guilt. We don't want Scarfey hanging around because he thinks we miss him. His body will

cover with mildew and grass roots and those little black bugs I don't
know the name of. His parts will split off and spin themselves into dirt.

We should plant a carrot patch there. That was my dad's idea. We
didn't do it because it seemed too gross.

## SCENE 5

*The sound of a hammer.*

LIESEL: Mr. Fancy Pants charges by the hour. Do you think he's stalling? I
think he's trying to get us to pay for a second and maybe even third hour.

MARCY: I can't tell.

LIESEL: You mean you don't know or you won't say?

MARCY: It hasn't even been two hours.

LIESEL: You need to put on real clothes.

MARCY: I'm not going anywhere.

LIESEL: Well that's just it, you should go somewhere.

MARCY: Not today.

LIESEL: I'm definitely going back to Omaha you know. I'm going back next
week.

MARCY: That's good.

LIESEL: I'm taking the kitchen table. You're gonna have to buy a new one.

MARCY: OK.

LIESEL: I'm taking Dad's car.

MARCY: . . . Fine.

LIESEL: My point being of course, that nothing is gonna hang around here
forever. *(Noticing the hammering has stopped.)* And I am not paying for a
third hour. It's a fence for God's sake, not the Taj Mahal.

## SCENE 6

LIESEL: Yes, this is my father, the asshole. He was good with children and bad
with money. No wait I'm sorry that's wrong. He was bad with children
and bad with money.

He had seizures sometimes, mostly due to alcohol consumption and
I know for certain of at least three people who deeply despised him.

No that's not my mother, I don't know where the mother is. She's
most likely on the West Coast because rumor has it that she liked

horses, sunshine, and the Pacific Ocean. She also liked costume jewelry. She got half her collection from flea markets and the other half from dead relatives who knew her when she was a child. She didn't think to leave behind any of it for me or my sister or my dad.

Or for the brother. We had a brother once. I've been told he died just as he was leaving the mother's womb, unable to breathe the air of the Earth.

She took the jewelry but not us, that's what we think in our heads.

No, I didn't kill my father. No not a coffin, an urn. He wanted to be cremated and he wanted to be inside the ground. He loved this house. It was his favorite outfit. The thing he always wanted to wear. He was here long before I arrived and he'll be here long after I'm gone. Which by the way will be next week. No, I don't know specifically what killed him, but it was not me.

SCENE 7

*Robbie and Marcy in the chaise lounge.*

ROBBIE: Sometimes I do work for Winchester Cemetery, the old one, not the new one. My uncle hooked me up. You should see some of those old graves, you ever been out there? Nobody visits them anymore, it's The Cemetery That Nobody Visits. All the people who used to visit are dead now too. So really what's the point, right? I mean, you know after a certain number of years, I mean like 100 years or something, they should maybe think about recycling the land for the next group, you know? I mean, I don't mean that in like a disrespectful way. You know what I mean, right?

LIESEL: *(Enters with a check, she hands it to him.)* You did a nice job.

ROBBIE: It wasn't that complicated.

LIESEL: Well, thanks for your time.

*(Robbie walks. He stops.)*

ROBBIE: Hey, my uncle knew your dad. When they were in school. They went to school together.

LIESEL: Oh?

ROBBIE: Yeah. He hadn't seen him in a long time though. I guess like a lot of people hadn't right? I mean, you guys saw him.

MARCY: He had a home business.

LIESEL: He wasn't very social.

ROBBIE: Yeah, well, I'm sorry that he . . . OK, well, have a good afternoon.

LIESEL: Did you hear that? It wasn't that complicated? I told you he was stalling.

## SCENE 8

*Light change — night*

MARCY: Dad didn't talk about the brother. He acted like there wasn't even a brother at all. There was an accident and a slipup. An accident with the thing. That's how he said it. After the thing. Before the thing.

Dad would have dug his own hole if he could. He didn't want to leave here ever. I'm going to stay here he said. I'm here for good. He didn't even go to the grocery store. I would go and buy him cheese and donuts and beer and vodka. The store didn't card me even though I was only fourteen.

Then I got older, and then I looked older, but what's weird about that is that's when they started carding me. So I went to the convenience store around the corner and I didn't get carded, so that was my new place. The guy at the register used to mow our lawn. He was in love with my mom and that's why he didn't card me.

That's what Liesel says. That's what my dad said. He believed the cash register guy once slept with my mother. He might even believe that the dead brother was the cash register guy's baby. That's maybe what allowed him to call the brother "thing."

*(Blackout.)*

## SCENE 9

*Morning. Marcy sleeping on the chaise lounge. The grave is covered in red paint. Robbie enters. Marcy starts and sits up, pointing her camera.*

ROBBIE: It's me. It's just me. Don't kill me.

MARCY: *(Noticing the gravestone.)* Oh no.

ROBBIE: Looks like they got him again . . .

MARCY: Assholes.

ROBBIE: You're probably wondering why I'm here . . . I was on my way to work, and I figured you'd be out here . . . and . . . I wanted to ask you if maybe I could call you sometime. Or if you feel uncomfortable giving me your phone number, I could give you my phone number. I guess your sister already has my phone number, so I don't need to give it to you. Unless you want me to give it to you.

MARCY: Everything's rotting. Everything in the world is just a rotten rotten sack of shit!

(*Robbie watches her. Blackout.*)


SCENE 10


*Marcy sitting. Robbie pacing, examining the ground. He takes a picture with Marcy's camera.*

ROBBIE: This looks like a footprint. Probably a size 9. Do you know any guys with small feet?

MARCY: I don't know. I can't think of anybody.

ROBBIE: I can get these developed at the one-hour place. I'll take the film there for you if you want.

MARCY: I don't think we're going to find him. The person who did it.

ROBBIE: I'll help. I can stay up with you, or we can take shifts.

MARCY: The person who did it is invisible.

ROBBIE: Well, they left footprints —

MARCY: It's a spirit. An evil spirit. Who travels on wind. Who hates me and hates my dad. Who hates my whole family.

ROBBIE: Oh. Well . . . we don't know that for sure.

MARCY: I know it. I know it for sure.

ROBBIE: So, do you still want me to take pictures?


SCENE 11


LIESEL: I want to go on a Caribbean cruise. I want to see what all the excitement is about. I'm going to do it too. I don't care how much it costs.

My father didn't believe in vacations but I'm guessing you could've figured that out yourself. He was too busy stuffing himself to death. He was too busy not working. He was too busy fucking people over via the telephone.

His only friend was our dead dog. I am not kidding in any way when I say he would rather talk to our dead dog than to live people. My sister would actually open her ears to his unending stream of shit. Not me, I wouldn't. But she would. And he didn't care, he would come out to the backyard, out by the fence, and lay down on the ground and, I am still not kidding, he would speak into the earth. Oh Scarfey, and then muffled whispers. He thought he was so clever. He insisted on being alone, you couldn't even come out to check the temperature. He was an asshole. But then, I've said that before, haven't I? Then I may as well say it again. Asshole.

SCENE 12

*Marcy and Robbie as before.*

LIESEL: *(To Robbie.)* What are you doing here?

ROBBIE: Oh, just being a detective sort of, you know? I think you might need to get some paint remover for that. Um. I can pick some up if you don't have any.

LIESEL: *(Motioning to the gravestone.)* Interesting how he can ruin my day even when he's dead. Don't you think that's interesting?

MARCY: It's not his fault.

LIESEL: Oh please. You think decent people get their graves attacked?

MARCY: Nobody deserves to be attacked when they're dead.

LIESEL: That's really really not true. There's a long list of dead people who deserve to be attacked. And I know it's hard for you to accept, but he's on that list. Maybe even near the top.

MARCY: That's sickening for you to talk like that.

LIESEL: Sickening? Fucking around with demons is what's sickening, Marcy. You're nineteen years old. Ever consider the possibility of thinking about getting a job? Ever consider opening a newspaper or doing some Goddamn laundry? You know what's sickening? Sickening is someone who sits around in dirty clothes babysitting their dead asshole father's fucking grave.
*(She exits.)*

ROBBIE: I'll go get the paint remover.
*(He exits.)*

SCENE 13

MARCY: I know our family is marked. That was my dad's theory. He told me when I asked him. What's wrong with me? Why is this happening? See, there's a sign floating over our house. It's shaped like a crescent moon. It points at us. Points us out so that everybody knows where we live and who we are and what we deserve.

He told me right before he died. His face was blue and he kept puking. He would puke and speak and puke and speak. I took it all in because I knew it would be my last chance. I knew he was almost gone.

We sat in the moon, it was flowing through the window. Everything about him looked like paper. I touched his hand and it was so dry. It was like burnt crisp paper. He kept puking. I might have normally felt sick to my stomach to watch, but I didn't feel sick at all and I don't know why that is.

It's none of their beeswax. That's what my dad said. But people make it their beeswax anyway.

SCENE 14

*Liesel enters.*

LIESEL: I'm leaving. I'm leaving this house and I'm not coming back.

MARCY: That's fine.

LIESEL: The only reason I came back was to clean this place out. But I changed my mind. I don't want to clean it. It can burn up for all I care.

MARCY: I don't need your help.

LIESEL: You're going to get smothered here. I hope you know that.

*(Marcy silent.)*

LIESEL: You know what? I honestly do not care. You're totally right on that point. I do not care.

*(She exits. Silence. Robbie enters with a can of paint remover.)*

ROBBIE: I got it. I had some in my truck. I got everything in my truck. Yeah, really. I mean if you need any tools or anything, you don't even have to go to the hardware store.

*(Marcy is silent. Robbie walks to the grave, opens the can.)*

ROBBIE: Hey, don't worry. I'm gonna get those photos developed and take 'em to the cops. I'm gonna talk to a few people. Get it figured out. I can tell you that much, it will get figured out. You can't just let something like this slide, you know? It's really sacrilegious, what these guys are doing. If you think about it.

*(He wipes at the grave.)*

ROBBIE: It probably just freaks people out a little bit. People probably don't feel all that comfortable with him here in your backyard . . . so they want to drive him away. That's just another perspective for you.

MARCY: He's not there.

ROBBIE: Huh?

MARCY: He's not there. He's not in the ground.

ROBBIE: How do you know?

MARCY: Because I put the container in and the container was empty. No ashes. No nothing.

ROBBIE: . . . So where is he?

MARCY: He disappeared. He blew away. He was stolen or he left. I don't know which one.

*(Silence. Robbie wipes at the grave.)*

ROBBIE: Did you report it?

MARCY: It's nothing to report. He was here, and now he's gone, and I don't know where he went.

*(Silence. Robbie wipes. After awhile: Blackout.)*

END OF PLAY

# Untitled #2

## Jim Gordon

*Untitled #2* was first performed in 2006 at The American
Theatre of Actors, in New York City. The cast:
Mr. Thompson — Mr. Joseph Mallon; Mr. Parker —
Mr. Jeffrey Sherman; Tornay — Mr. Jim Gordon.

# CHARACTERS

* MR. PARKER: a critic, forty to sixty
* MR. THOMPSON: another critic, forty to sixty
TORNAY: an artist, thirty-five to forty-five

*The part of Tornay and Voice-Over are performed by the same actor.*
* *The roles of Parker and Thompson can be played by any combination of men and women.*

# SETTING

An art gallery

# TIME

The present

# SYNOPSIS

Two "art critics" view a painting by one of their favorite artists and come to strikingly different opinions as to the meaning of the work. Caught up in a fever of contrasting artistic and political views they come close to fisticuffs before the artist sets them straight.

• • •

*We are in an art gallery. Mr. Thompson is sitting on a bench and looking downstage at a painting displayed on an easel. The subject of the painting cannot be seen by the audience. Mr. Parker enters the room and crosses to the painting. He examines it, and steps back. He moves forward again for a more detailed examination. He becomes aware he is standing in Parker's sight line and turns:*

THOMPSON: Oh, I'm so sorry, I didn't see you sitting there.
PARKER: It's all right, I don't mind sharing.
*(A pause, as Thompson goes back to admiring the painting.)*
Quite wonderful, isn't it?
THOMPSON: *(Good-naturedly.)* "Wonderful?" Bit of an understatement, don't you think?
PARKER: Yes. Yes, you're right, it's more than that.
THOMPSON: You're familiar with Tornay's work.
PARKER: Brilliant artist, absolutely brilliant.

THOMPSON: This piece, how would you rate it, compared with his earlier paintings, I mean?

PARKER: More mature, I'd say. More . . . more passionate.

THOMPSON: Passionate! Yes, I like that — passionate! Did you see his Baltimore show?

PARKER: No, I didn't have the opp —

THOMPSON: *(Interrupting.)* Marvelous stuff, absolutely marvelous . . . but this . . . this is his best, no question. *(He extends his hand.)* Thompson's the name.

PARKER: *(Shaking Thompson's hand.)* Parker's mine.

THOMPSON: *(Points at the empty seat next to Parker.)* May I?

PARKER: Please.

*(He sits.)*

THOMPSON: A pleasure to meet someone able to recognize Tornay's genius.

PARKER: A woman was here earlier, hadn't the faintest idea what she was looking at, poor thing. She told her companion it was a landscape!

THOMPSON: *A LANDSCAPE?*

PARKER: Can you imagine?

THOMPSON: *A LANDSCAPE. MY GOD!*

PARKER: I'd have suggested she read the catalogue description, *(He points at the catalogue he's holding.)* but I wasn't sure she could read.
*(They both laugh.)*

THOMPSON: They ran out of catalogues, might I see yours.
*(Parker hands him his brochure. He reads.)*
"A reductive sensibility pervades the entire painting, although of abstract construction, a radical aesthetic of formal clarity dispersed with a complexity of simple truths dominate the subject. Tornay has suffused *Untitled #2* with a sensitivity that illustrates the artist's desire to explore a simple reality while instituting a new universal language that blends harmoniously in conjunction with an increasingly nonreferential, elemental form." *(He looks at the painting. After a moment . . .)* Yes . . . yes, I'd agree with that.

PARKER: Though it's strange he refers to the work as abstract.

THOMPSON: Sorry?

PARKER: Well, his message couldn't be clearer, could it?

THOMPSON: Exactly what I was thinking. *(He nudges Parker.)* Great minds and all that, hey?

PARKER: Although, I must admit, I don't like that label.

THOMPSON: Oh? *Untitled #2?* You don't like it?

PARKER: Can't say I do.

THOMPSON: What would you call it?

PARKER: Well, I'm not so presumptuous to think I could —

THOMPSON: No, no please, I'd be interested in hearing your thoughts.

PARKER: Well . . . peace . . . yes, peace, is what I'd call it. I think that would be an accurate description.

THOMPSON: *(Beat.)* Peace?

PARKER: And, if I had my way, I'd hang it in the United Nations. It says more than all those diplomats with their high-sounding —

THOMPSON: *(Interrupting.)* Peace? You think the painting represents peace?

PARKER: Why yes, yes, I do.

THOMPSON: Hmmmm.

PARKER: You don't?

THOMPSON: It's funny.

PARKER: What is?

THOMPSON: How two intelligent people can look at a work and come to such divergent interpretations.

PARKER: Well . . . perhaps peace is a bit too strong. . . tranquility might be a better —

THOMPSON: Tranquility? No I don't think so. No, not tranquility either.

PARKER: What then?

THOMPSON: Of course, it's only my opinion . . .

PARKER: No, please . . .

THOMPSON: *(He's up.)* Well, look at those colors . . . the reds, the oranges . . . the boldness of the brushstrokes; this is an angry work, my friend.

PARKER: Angry? That's what you see — anger?

THOMPSON: Very much so. What you're seeing here is a call for confrontation, a call for war.

PARKER: *WAR?*

THOMPSON: No question. I'm afraid you've misread Tornay's message.

PARKER: *(He's up.)* But the softness of line, the lack of hard edges, the blending of the clouds . . .

THOMPSON: *Clouds?* Where do you see clouds?

PARKER: There, in the corner, those masses of gray . . .

THOMPSON: You think those are clouds?

PARKER: What else?

THOMPSON: *(Laughing.)* Pardon me for laughing, Mr. Parker, but those aren't clouds — that's smoke!

PARKER: *Smoke?*

THOMPSON: No question.

PARKER: *Smoke?* From what?

THOMPSON: The bombs, my friend, the bombs.

PARKER: *BOMBS?*

(*He studies the painting. After a moment.*)

No. No, I'm afraid it is not I who is mistaken.

THOMPSON: Well, as I said, it's only my opinion.

PARKER: As it is mine.

THOMPSON: (*Beat.*) Of course *my* opinion is based on my extensive background in the field of art and art appreciation.

PARKER: Oh, you're an educator?

THOMPSON: No.

PARKER: Art historian?

THOMPSON: No.

PARKER: Then you're an artist?

THOMPSON: Why no, I . . .

PARKER: (*Interrupting.*) An adult education course, perhaps.

THOMPSON: My education is more informal, more intuitive.

PARKER: Oh, I see.

THOMPSON: No . . . no, I don't think you do.

PARKER: Why don't we just agree to disagree, and leave it at that, shall we?

THOMPSON: I suppose we'll have to, won't we?

(*They both stare at the painting, but, after a moment, unable to contain themselves, they blurt out — simultaneously.*)

PARKER: *WAR?*                THOMPSON: *PEACE?*

PARKER: For God sake, the man is a pacifist; understanding and compassion resonate throughout his paintings.

THOMPSON: Until 9/11.

PARKER: 9/11? Are you suggesting 9/11 changed him from pacifist to a militant?

THOMPSON: I'm not suggesting anything, *I'm telling you!*

PARKER: Oh, I see, and there's no possibility you might be mistaken?

THOMPSON: None!

PARKER: Not a chance you might be wrong?

THOMPSON: No, and if you had seen his Baltimore exhibition, you'd know what I'm talking about. I'm afraid *you've* been out of touch.

PARKER: And you've obviously been influenced by your political leanings.

THOMPSON: *What do you know of my politics?*

PARKER: I think it's safe to assume they're right of center.

THOMPSON: Now wait a minute —

PARKER: Next you'll be telling me Tornay's in favor of what we're doing over there.

THOMPSON: By "over there," I assume you mean the war?

PARKER: Well, at least you have that right.

THOMPSON: Tornay's position on our participation in that conflict is quite clear; it's right there, in front of you, if you would only open your eyes.

PARKER: I beg your pardon, Mr. Thompson, but my eyes are open, *wide open*, and what I see are arms, arms and hands stretched toward the heavens and pleading for peace.

THOMPSON: *Arms? Hands? Where do you see arms and hands?*

PARKER: *(Parker crosses quickly toward the painting. Pointing.)* There, right there. Are you blind?

THOMPSON: *(He laughs.)* ARMS . . . HANDS?

PARKER: Yes, and they're pleading. No, they're praying, praying for sanity in a world gone mad.

THOMPSON: *THOSE AREN'T ARMS, THEY'RE MISSILE LAUNCHERS!*

PARKER: *MISSILE LAUNCHERS?* That's the most ridiculous —

THOMPSON: *(Interrupting.)* Although, I'm pleased to hear you believe in the power of prayer, your type usually don't.

PARKER: My *TYPE?*

THOMPSON: You know what I mean.

PARKER: I certainly do not! Please explain that remark.

THOMPSON: I'm having enough trouble trying to explain the painting.

PARKER: It's obvious to me that you know less about this piece than that woman who was here earlier.

THOMPSON: And your interpretation is as bizarre as hers.

PARKER: I'm not going to continue this discussion

*(He rises to leave.)*

THOMPSON: Typical liberal.

PARKER: What did you say?

THOMPSON: You heard me.

PARKER: Fascist

THOMPSON: War!

PARKER: Peace!

THOMPSON: *WAR!*

PARKER: *PEACE!*

OFFSTAGE VOICE: *GENTLEMEN? QUIET! PLEASE!*

*(Parker and Thompson look off toward the Voice. After a beat, they*

*continue — same level of anger, but their words are spoken quietly — almost a whisper.)*

THOMPSON: War!

PARKER: Peace!

THOMPSON: War!

PARKER: Peace!

THOMPSON: *(He races toward the painting and points. He's back to his normal voice.)* What is that?

PARKER: What is what?

THOMPSON: *That! That! Right there, what is that?*

PARKER: A rainbow.

THOMPSON: *(He begins to laugh uncontrollably.) A RAINBOW? My God, I don't believe you, you are too funny.*

PARKER: What then?

THOMPSON: It's the vapor trail from the jet that dropped the bomb that's caused those clouds of smoke. That's what that is! What Tornay has given us here, is a confirmation of our leader's decision that right is might. *Right is might! That is this painting's message, nothing less, and God bless Tornay for realizing it.*

PARKER: Tornay has giving us a message all right. No, he's given us a warning! He's telling us were we are headed if we refuse to challenge the hair-brained miscalculations of our current leadership and the misguided morons who support them.

THOMPSON: *Morons?*

PARKER: *Yes, morons, and people of your ilk.*

THOMPSON: Ilk? *ILK?*

PARKER: *You're an ignorant . . . an ignorant . . . ignorant . . .*
*(He can't get it out.)*

THOMPSON: What's the matter, Mr. Liberal, don't have the guts to say it. Spit it out! What . . . ignorant what?

PARKER: You . . . you . . . *IGNORANT RIGHT-WING SHITHEAD!*
*(Thompson, slowly, begins to remove his jacket. He's preparing to fight. Parker does likewise, and they lay their clothing on the bench.)*

THOMPSON: Wait a second. Isn't that Tornay?

PARKER: By God it is he.

THOMPSON: Unfortunately for you.
*(Tornay enters from Upper Left and crosses behind and in between Thompson and Parker. Thompson and Parker are looking upstage at Tornay and He's looking downstage toward his painting.)*

PARKER: Pardon me sir . . . THOMPSON: Mr. Tornay . . .

TORNAY: Yes gentlemen, what is it?

THOMPSON: Mr. Tornay, I would like you to set this man straight on something —

PARKER: Me? Set me straight? I like that. Mr. Tornay, please tell this fellow —

*(Tornay has noticed something.)*

TORNAY: A moment, please.

*(Tornay crosses downstage between Parker and Thompson and stops in front of Untitled #2. He shakes his head in frustration as he notices his painting has been placed wrong side up. He takes the work and reverses its position, then steps back to admire it, then crosses upstage and below Thompson and Parker; at this point, Tornay's back is to the painting. Parker and Thompson are staring in disbelief at what they have just witnessed.)*

Now gentlemen, what can I do for you?

*(After a moment, Thompson and Parker slowly and uncomfortably reach for their coats. Parker exits stage Left as Thompson exits stage Right. Tornay watches both men exit. Puzzled, he turns to look at Untitled #2. After a moment, he shrugs, and the lights go quickly to black.)*

END OF PLAY

# The Deal

## KATE McCAMEY

*The Deal* was originally commissioned and produced for
REVENGE 2 by The Drilling Company, artistic director
Hamilton Clancy. It was presented at 78th Street Theatre Lab
in New York City December 3, 2005, directed by Richard
Mover, stage managed by Billie Davis, with sets by Rebecca
Lord, lights by Miriam Nilofa Crowe, with the following cast:
Buck — Richard Mover; Mike — Michael Ornstein;
Todd — Randy Noojin.

CHARACTERS

> BUCK: a lawyer (thirties plus)
> MIKE: twenties, filmmaker
> TODD: twenties, filmmaker

SETTING

> A lawyer's office

• • •

*A lawyer's office, one desk, two chairs, and a phone. Mike and Todd are facing off with Buck in the middle.*

MIKE: You tell him I wouldn't piss down his throat if his heart was on fire! How dare he accuse me of ruining the integrity of the project?!

TODD: Would you tell him it's not an accusation, it's the literal truth.

MIKE: You tell him he's gotta be fucking kidding me!

TODD: Oh, believe me, I'm as serious as cancer.

MIKE: No, you are a cancer!

TODD: C'mon, I'm just a filmmaker . . .

MIKE: Filmmaker! You're a fucking thief!

TODD: Be careful of what you say, my lawyer is present.

MIKE: He's my lawyer too!

BUCK: I haven't been retained yet. Now can one of you, calmly, tell me what caused this, shall we say, schism?

MIKE/TODD: Well, he, it all started . . .

BUCK: Gentlemen, please, one at a time. Mike?

MIKE: He wants to do some re-enactment shit, like they do on the History channel! Put actors in cheesy costumes and make them run around looking like Ghengis Kahn or some crap.

TODD: I never said that!

MIKE: I saved your e-mails . . .

TODD: I said manipulate the situation to balance it out. All docs are doing it now. Come on nothing is really real anymore. Even reality shows aren't real. What is reality anyway? A fleeting moment of truth that gets altered in a memory, and usually is, by the way. So why can't we manufacture moments? He doesn't know the first thing about telling a story.

BUCK: Story? I thought you were making a movie?

MIKE: Documentary, documenting real people with grassroots issues in the expanding global economy. And you are so full of shit, reality, what is real? Please! I'll give you some fucking reality, give me my camera and the footage I shot or . . .

TODD: Or what? See he's totally irrational, threatening me like a . . .

MIKE: Like a what? What!

BUCK: OK guys, time out. You're wasting my time and your money. *(To Mike.)* Why don't you step out there, Vicky'll get you a bottle of water, relax, OK? OK?

MIKE: Why do I have to leave?

BUCK: Because you're thirsty.

MIKE: Oh, OK.

*(Mike leaves the room.)*

BUCK: Now about this . . . Rolex?

TODD: Bolex.

BUCK: Todd, tell me, is this Bolex really Mike's personal property? . . . Todd?

TODD: Yes sir . . .

BUCK: Please, call me Buck.

TODD: OK, Buck. Look, I was just holding it, hoping to get him to shoot the mass exodus from the financial center the way I see it. He thinks it shouldn't be staged. But it has to in order to get the pathos, it's our grand finale. You know how hard it is to come up with an ending? Jesus! We've got gold in the can but we still have to shoot the dark side, we don't have a middle and he's giving me shit about the end!

BUCK: So get someone else to shoot it. You shoot it.

TODD: I, well I thought about that, but, his camera work is, well they call him Mr. Eyeball. His whole visual sense is like unique. When we did *Kill da Wabbit* in college — they screamed! I mean he made blood look so damn real. People said we were better than Sam Raimi and Bruce Campbell!

BUCK: Whoa whoa pal, come back. Be here now. You with me?

TODD: Yeah, sure. I got you. I'm back.

BUCK: Now why don't you tell me what you want out of this deal?

TODD: What do I want?

BUCK: Be clear . . .

TODD: I am clear, so very clear. I can see it like glass, really clean, smudge free museum glass . . .

BUCK: So?

TODD: I want to be the sole director of this film. No "shared" credit shit. I have the vision, I've written and rewritten most of the script, I need creative control. That is what my expectation is. And I'm not going to let a twenty-year friendship stand in the way dammit!

BUCK: Ah yes, you'll do well in the movie business.

TODD: You see, Mike's problem is, he means well but he has no follow-through, he has no idea how to implement a deal. This thing will sit on a shelf and turn into celluloid dust if it were left in his hands. This film has to be finished, the people must witness this film. I hate to say this but my partner, well, he's an incompetent idealist.

BUCK: An idealist?

TODD: 'Fraid so.

BUCK: Any other frailties?

TODD: Frailties?

BUCK: You gotta go for the weak link in his chain. What is his weak link?

TODD: Well, he's weak. I mean, you know, gullible. People take advantage of him all the time.

BUCK: Good we can work with that. Now does he have any money, assets?

TODD: Assets? If it weren't for his girlfriend, he'd be out on the street. He's a lost soul really, but she does have a rent-controlled loft downtown. Actually he's very lucky to have Silvia. But whatever, why? You think I should offer him a buy out?

BUCK: That is a potential solution, throw money at the problem. How much you got?

TODD: I don't think a buyout is an option.

BUCK: Let me ask you something, did you guys sign an agreement, a contract? Anything like that?

TODD: Ah, no, no we haven't quite gotten around to it yet, is that a problem?

BUCK: Actually it might work in your favor at the moment. You say you have the film in your possession?

TODD: Yes.

BUCK: Well, he's got no money, what's he gonna do, sue you?

TODD: Yes, I see your point.

(Mike peeks in holding a bottle of water.)

MIKE: I'm better now, can I come back in?

BUCK: Sure, we were just talking about you, weren't we?

MIKE: Oh yeah? What were you saying?

BUCK: Todd here was just telling me what a wonderful and supportive girl-friend you have.

MIKE: Really?

TODD: Sure, Silvie's great.

MIKE: Yeah, she is, she's gonna be a good editor, you've seen the footage? Of course you have, because you have it in your possession.

*(Buck is reviewing some notes. They sit in an uncomfortable silence.)*

TODD: You know, I think I could use some water too. I'm gonna get some water, you want any?

BUCK: No thanks.

MIKE: I'm good.

*(Todd steps out.)*

BUCK: *(Looking over notes.)* I'm gonna quote you here, "your equipment has been stolen, your work, stolen, the 50/50 collaboration dissolved. You want full ownership"? I get that right?

MIKE: Yes. I want my Bolex back, and I didn't say full ownership of the project, it's more like I'm, I just want to do the film right. It's important, people need to see this . . .

BUCK: Of course it's important. You wouldn't be here if it weren't. Now, when did you first suspect your opponent of malfeasance?

MIKE: My opponent?

BUCK: What's his name? Todd?

MIKE: Todd yeah. We always work as a team, I just don't get it. We could always talk about stuff, you know? Sex, politics, joke about anything, people, sex . . .

BUCK: You wanna marry the guy or sue him?

MIKE: Uh, no sir, no I don't.

BUCK: Please, call me Buck.

MIKE: Oh, OK, Buck, I don't know, I just don't feel right about screwing him.

BUCK: Sure you do. Somebody fucks you, you gotta fuck them back ten times harder, trust me, I know where of I speak.

MIKE: I guess so, but I, just, you know . . .

BUCK: You know what? You need to empower yourself here. You let this guy walk all over you, take advantage of your good nature and generosity and where did it get you?

MIKE: Ah, ripped off?

BUCK: Fist-fucked to the armpit my friend! And now he wants to take the whole project from you? Rip it from your womb and raise it as "his movie." I think you want more than just a camera, you want financial compensation. Am I right! C'mon, am I right?

MIKE: You really think I can screw him?

BUCK: Sue, sue, not screw, but yes I think you should go for the gold, why just try to get your footage back . . .

MIKE: And camera.

BUCK: And your camera, let's go for the whole canoodle.

MIKE: Canoodle? I don't think I want to do that.

BUCK: I think you do. We got to plan our attack. I say we go for the Achilles tendon.

MIKE: I guess if you think so.

BUCK: So what is it?

MIKE: What is what?

BUCK: Where is he vulnerable?

MIKE: Oh, well, he quit drinking and smoking, the guy's a wreck.

BUCK: I don't think you quite understand, we need something a little more substantial. Skeletons in the closet, dark meaty shit, you got anything like that for me?

MIKE: OK, I got you, he used to sell pot.

BUCK: Used to is no good. Let me ask you something, how much you think he's worth?

MIKE: Would that be day rate or weekly?

BUCK: I'm talking assets, a house, family money, trusts anything like that?

MIKE: Money? That mooch? No, you kiddin', he was crashing on my couch until a week ago. Hell he owes me for his share of the expenses.

BUCK: Expenses?

MIKE: For the project, I'm already out of pocket something like three grand . . .

BUCK: Are you nuts?! Rule number one, never, EVER, use your own money on a movie. Never. Especially a documentary!

MIKE: I know, I know that, but it has to be made, no doubt about it, it's too important to use the lack of money as an excuse . . .

BUCK: How did you guys get this far?

MIKE: Uh, well . . .

*(Todd peeks in.)*

TODD: I, uh, I gotta be honest . . .

BUCK: Not the way to a peaceful resolution.

TODD: We've been going around in circles.

BUCK: Yes and I'm afraid your hour is up.

TODD: But we haven't resolved anything.

BUCK: You guys can't afford another hour.

TODD: Jesus Christ, it's all about money with you!

BUCK: No it is not just about money.

MIKE: But you keep bringing it up . . .

TODD: He wanted to know how much money you had . . .

MIKE: Get out. He said the same to me . . .

TODD: What'd you tell him?

MIKE: I said you were broke.

TODD: Oh, good.

MIKE: Yeah, so what's up with that?

TODD: There is more to life than just money.

BUCK: Can you be more specific?

MIKE: Inner peace for example?

BUCK: I am a conduit for restitution and inner peace of mind.

TODD: Yeah, well you charge a helluva lot for it.

BUCK: Money is value attributed, the universal system by which we gauge everything.

MIKE: Money is the root of evil.

BUCK: Is it? So why are you here?

TODD: I don't know any more.

MIKE: This is bullshit.

BUCK: You're here because you want power. He wants power over you, and you want power over him. And to think you have the audacity to use this do-goody documentary as a tool to play God. Shame on you both.

TODD: What kind of crap is that? God?

MIKE: He's crazy. I don't want to stand here and be lectured to by some fucking shyster.

BUCK: Oh, I'm a shyster? And what, my friend are you?

MIKE: I'm a human fucking being who can sleep at night, how do you sleep? You, you're like the . . . the Devil incarnate.

BUCK: You wouldn't know the Devil if it fucked you in the ass! You, my friends are little puppets dancing on the end of a long string of avarice, you and everybody else. You're the reason why I'm here. Why I do what I do. Human nature is the only thing on this planet that is inherently evil. Think about it, puppies aren't evil, sea urchins aren't evil, even snakes aren't evil. Simple beings whose sole purpose is to eat, sleep, and procreate. People, your "People" on the other hand are rotten, wretched huddled masses, condemned to their own hell because they are blessed with the awareness of their own mortality. Yeah, that's right. You know you're gonna die. And you need to create a buffer between you and your inevitable death. You know what that buffer is?

TODD/MIKE: Uh, no . . .

BUCK: Stuff. People need to have more stuff than the other guy, see someone even worse off than them so they can say, "Ah, but there for the grace of God go I!" Yeah, that's right, how many cars and homes you own, how many jaw-dropping model babes you can parade around on your arms and be seen at the hot new restaurant eating hundred-dollar plates of nothing. How much clout you have. And that is a fact. And if you tell me you don't subscribe to the archetypes, you're full of shit.

*(Todd and Mike look at each other.)*

TODD: Meant to be?

MIKE: It's what we need.

TODD: Hey Buck, that was really . . . Could you do that again? On camera?

BUCK: What? What?

MIKE: Your point of view about human nature? It's so fucked up but so true.

TODD: The issue about needing an underclass. That rounds out the theme really beautifully.

MIKE: And the fabric part too.

BUCK: C'mon, what are you talking about?

TODD: Are you interested in being in our documentary? We need you to balance it out . . .

BUCK: C'mon, you can't shit a shitter . . .

MIKE: No really.

*(Mike fiddles with his camera.)*

TODD: This is no snow job, I mean it, we need more conflict in our story and I really think you are it.

BUCK: Me? No you got the wrong guy . . .

TODD: No man, really, I've interviewed many people and to find someone who is real and passionate and can communicate it so eloquently is rare.

BUCK: Well you did hit a nerve . . .

MIKE: Maybe over there. Better light.

TODD: No right here. Yes, starting with evil . . .

BUCK: Evil?

MIKE: The fabric needs me, people are rotten . . .

BUCK: Oh yeah, I was responding to your accusation.

MIKE: You want me to cue you?

BUCK: Cue me?

MIKE: Evil! Money! Money evil!

TODD: Hold it, cut, cut. I'm sorry. This is a little stagy. You know Mike, I been mulling over what you said and you're right we shouldn't stage anything, it has to be real.

MIKE: Yeah I been thinking too and it's a lot of bullshit, this is gold.

TODD: Yes, but you had a point, real people, real shit. Keep it spontaneous.

MIKE: But this is totally spontaneous.

TODD: OK, let's do this thing. You'd sign a release and be in this movie?

BUCK: I don't really understand what kind of part you want me to play in this.

TODD: To be yourself, give us your viewpoint of how this whole crazy world functions.

BUCK: You really want my point of view?

TODD: Absolutely.

MIKE: No doubt.

BUCK: I gotta tell you, you guys have really impressed me.

MIKE/TODD: Really?

BUCK: You think on the spot. That's good and you've obviously got a real mission, you really care about this. Set aside your differences uniting for the common good for your little project. That alone is gold, metaphorically speaking.

TODD: Of course, of course.

MIKE: Yeah, yeah.

BUCK: You don't wanna screw each other do you? No. You want to make a difference. And you know something? So do I, I wanna make a difference too. And not just to my 401(k).

TODD: Well, here's your chance.

BUCK: How much you need to finish this picture?

TODD: The film? We're so close, we need access to the other agenda, the last scene . . .

MIKE: Five thousand?

BUCK: That is, well that's just insane. You can't even buy a bad idea for that. You're letting humility crush your spirit. Don't let that happen. It's a black hole spiral down, believe you me. I didn't get to where I am today by eating humble pie. You gotta be aggressive. Dare to be despised, that's what gets you respect. Ask and ye shall receive, but you gotta ask.

MIKE: Ten thousand?

BUCK: Demand.

TODD: We might have to pay some music royalties . . .

MIKE: Hey, you know about music royalties?

BUCK: I wrote the book! I'm the reason you gotta pay those two old biddies for "Happy Birthday"!

MIKE: Yeah, how much they cost?

BUCK: More than you got.

TODD: Then we want to go to Sundance —

MIKE: And Slamdance.

BUCK: Doable, doable, what else? How about a celebrity narrator? You need somebody big, an icon like John Wayne.

MIKE: But he's dead.

BUCK: Yeah, but don't let that stop you.

TODD: With a real budget we could get Uma to narrate . . .

BUCK: Uma Thurman?

TODD: Woman narrators are hot now. Mike knows her personally.

BUCK: You "know" Uma?

MIKE: Ah, yes, we e-mail jokes . . .

BUCK: How about Paris Hilton, she'd be good.

MIKE: Who?

TODD: She'll up the budget considerably.

BUCK: By how much?

TODD: A hundred grand at least.

MIKE: Fuck it, get Morgan Freeman, people will watch anything if he's talking.

BUCK: That is so true. Even penguins. What else?

TODD: I can't believe, are you, serious?

BUCK: I want a credit.

MIKE: Above the line credit!

BUCK: EXECUTIVE PRODUCER!

TODD: Absolutely.

BUCK: You know something? I wanna see this movie of yours, ours. I really do. I want to make this real, for you, me, the world. Everybody should see this movie. You know why? Because it's gonna be fucking great! Finally a balanced documentary. Hell it's gonna create it's own genre! You get me Paris and this will be hotter than global warming. You wanna be insiders, players, right?

TODD: Uh, yeah . . .

MIKE: Yeah.

BUCK: Hey you, Mr. Eyeball, you rolling? We're going to show the people that if you work hard enough you can do whatever you want. It's the American dream. We might just change the world.

TODD: And how will we do that?

BUCK: Well, first we get people off their couch-potato butts, the armchair activists with their petitions and their hyperbole away from the Internet and into the workforce. We give them a direction, a sense of purpose that leads to an absolute, irrefutable, nonrefundable belief system. And for those who don't comply, the insurgents, if you will, they get routed out. Now there's your mass exodus.

TODD: How do you define *insurgent?*

BUCK: You know, there has been a lot of talk about increasing border security, tightening up, clamping down, chips implanted, satellite monitoring, but that's, well that's just the tip, the nipple. Like anything colossal, it starts out small. It starts with you. Yes you. You are the pulse, you owe it to the sheep to guide them. You keep your ear to the ground, nose to grindstone, watch, listen, tighten the borders of your mind. Yeah, it's that small. You ever see a neutrino? Of course not, they're really, really, small, you can't see them, but trust me, they're there.

*(Todd and Mike look at each other, then at Buck.)*

BUCK: Now who should I make a check out to?

*(They both look at each other.)*

BUCK: You incorporated? LLC? DBA? A name? Title of the film? I have an idea for that by the way.

TODD: Um . . . ah . . . this is not quite what we . . .

*(Buck plops a very large wad of cash on the desk and pushes it toward Todd.)*

BUCK: Were you saying something? I will need a fiduciary report of incurred expenses, and of course the tape.

MIKE: *(He videos the cash.)* Wow. You want this tape?

BUCK: Yes that tape.

TODD: The film business is a risky investment.

BUCK: You kidding me? By the time we're through, they'll be making up adjectives about you two.

MIKE: Uh, here.

*(Mike reluctantly hands him the tape from the camera as Todd fondles the cash.)*

BUCK: Now we are in business, brothers in sin-ema!

MIKE: You might as well be flushing that down the toilet.

TODD: Sshh.

MIKE: What does this mean?

TODD: It means we can make our film.

MIKE: This movie won't make a dime, you know that?

BUCK: *(Referring to the tape.)* All this IS binding by the way. Now get out there and rock that casbah!

MIKE AND TODD: OK. Thank you? We're going. Rockin'.

*(They both edge out the door.)*

MIKE: Fuck it, let's shoot on 35mm.TODD: That'll look so good, oh my God, we gotta get Pascal to edit. I know he's busy but for the right price . . .

MIKE: But, Silvie is editing. She's already done half the fucking work.

TODD: Your girlfriend will make a fine editor one day, but you know she doesn't have the street cred we need.

MIKE: Street cred Mr. Hollywood! Why don't you get Paris Hilton to edit the fucking thing . . .

TODD: Shut up!

MIKE: Give me my camera . . .

TODD: Hey, fuck you . . .

END OF PLAY

# Come Into the Garden, Maud

DON NIGRO

*Come Into the Garden, Maud* was first produced at Shadowbox Cabaret in Columbus, Ohio, with the following cast: John — Mark Slack; Phoebe — Carrie Lynn McDonald; Jill — Michelle Daniels. It was directed by Colleen Dalton.

## CHARACTERS

    JOHN: twenty-seven
    PHOEBE: twenty-one
    JILL: twenty-four

## SETTING

Stage right, a chair with a small wooden table on which are a lamp and telephone in John's house. Stage left, the same, with a phone book, in Phoebe's house. The rest of the stage is in darkness.

## PLAYWRIGHT'S NOTE

Late one night in Malvern, in 1993, the phone rang, and it was a slightly inebriated man who announced, with no preamble whatsoever, "Your cat's in my garden." It took me a long time to convince him that he had the wrong number, as he was, in fact, as I was finally able to establish, attempting to reach a relative of mine with the same last name whose cat kept relieving himself in this man's garden. We finally straightened it out, but for some reason the incident stayed with me. There was something rather unsettling about the ability of a total stranger to make a noise in my kitchen in the middle of the night and thrust one unexpectedly into a violent disagreement about the nature of reality — that is, whether or not there was a cat, or a garden, and if it was my cat, and if my cat was indeed in his garden. It seemed to me to be a rather profound question, somehow. The title is from Tennyson's long poem, *Maud,* part of which I set to music for James Joyce to sing in *Lucia Mad.*

•   •   •

*Phoebe turns on the light by her telephone. She wears a rather fetching nightie. She sits, looks up a number in the book, dials. John's telephone rings. After a bit, John appears, wearing only pajama bottoms, turns on his lamp, and picks up the phone.*

JOHN: Hello?

PHOEBE: Your cat's in my garden.

JOHN: What?

PHOEBE: Your cat's in my garden.

JOHN: I think you've got the wrong number.

PHOEBE: No I don't.

JOHN: Yes you do.

PHOEBE: Is this the Murphy residence?

JOHN: Yes.

PHOEBE: Your cat's in my garden.

JOHN: Who are you trying to reach?

PHOEBE: Murphy.

JOHN: Well, there's about a hundred Murphys in the phone book. You've just got the wrong one.

PHOEBE: I don't think so.

JOHN: I'm afraid you do. Good-bye.

*(He hangs up, turns off the light, and goes, as Phoebe redials. John's phone rings. He returns, turns on the light, picks up the phone.)*
Hello?

PHOEBE: Your cat's in my garden.

JOHN: My cat is not in your garden.

PHOEBE: Yes she is. I can see her out my window.

JOHN: Maybe you can see a cat out your window, but it's not mine, because I don't have a cat.

PHOEBE: Yes you do.

JOHN: No I don't.

PHOEBE: I know you have a cat, because it's in my garden.

JOHN: Look, it's four o'clock in the morning, and you have the wrong number, so would you please stop calling me?

PHOEBE: Your cat is in my garden. Don't you care?

JOHN: NO, I DON'T CARE, BECAUSE I DON'T HAVE ANY GOD-DAMNED CAT. I HATE CATS, AND I HATE YOU, SO STOP BOTHERING ME.

*(He slams down the phone, turns off the light, goes. Phoebe redials. John's phone rings. He returns, turns on the light, and picks up the phone.)*
WHAT?

PHOEBE: That was very rude. Why would you hate me? What did I ever do to you?

JOHN: You keep calling me at four o'clock in the morning.

PHOEBE: Only because your cat's in my garden.

JOHN: MY CAT IS NOT IN YOUR GARDEN.

PHOEBE: I think you're in a serious state of denial.

JOHN: WILL YOU PLEASE JUST LEAVE ME ALONE?

PHOEBE: *(Starting to cry.)* Well, I'm sorry. I was just worried about your cat. You don't have to yell at me.

*(She cries.)*

JOHN: Don't cry. I didn't mean to yell at you. I'm really tired, and you've just called me three times in the middle of the night to tell me my cat's in your garden.

PHOEBE: So you admit it.

JOHN: No, I don't admit it.

PHOEBE: You just said your cat was in my garden.

JOHN: No, I just — what number were you calling?

PHOEBE: Well, yours, of course.

JOHN: Which Murphy were you calling?

PHOEBE: I was calling you.

JOHN: What's my name?

PHOEBE: You mean you don't know?

JOHN: Yes, I know.

PHOEBE: Then what are you asking me for?

JOHN: Look, Miss —

PHOEBE: Phoebe.

JOHN: Phoebe. That's a lovely name, Phoebe.

PHOEBE: Thank you.

JOHN: The problem is, I don't know anybody named Phoebe.

PHOEBE: You know me.

JOHN: No, I don't know you.

PHOEBE: Yes you do. Your cat's in my garden.

*(Pause.)*

JOHN: What is my cat doing in your garden, Phoebe?

PHOEBE: Wait a minute. Let me look. *(She peers downstage through an invisible window.)* It's really dark out there. When I first called, she was having sexual intercourse. Well, I presume that's what it was. There was certainly a hell of a lot of screaming going on. Cats are a lot like people, don't you think? You really might want to consider getting her fixed.

JILL: *(Entering, wearing the tops of John's pajamas.)* Who are you talking to?

JOHN: Nobody.

PHOEBE: What?

JILL: It must be somebody.

JOHN: It's just some girl who says my cat's in her garden.

PHOEBE: Who's that? Mrs. Murphy?

JOHN: No, it's not.

PHOEBE: You're not cheating on Mrs. Murphy, are you?

JOHN: There is no Mrs. Murphy.

JILL: Johnny, who is that?

JOHN: It's Phoebe.

JILL: Phoebe who?

JOHN: I don't know.

PHOEBE: So you're sleeping with a woman you're not married to? Is that it?

JOHN: Yes, Phoebe, that's it, that is exactly it, I am sleeping with a woman I'm not married to. I hope that doesn't shock you too much.

PHOEBE: I just hope Mrs. Murphy doesn't find out.

JILL: You told me you weren't seeing anybody.

JOHN: I'm not seeing anybody.

PHOEBE: Then who is that woman?

JOHN: I wasn't talking to you, Phoebe. I was talking to Jill.

JILL: I want to know who this Phoebe is, and I want to know right now.

JOHN: It's a wrong number.

JILL: Then how do you know her name?

JOHN: We were just talking.

JILL: Why are you talking to a wrong number?

JOHN: Because she won't shut up.

JILL: Why don't you just hang up the phone?

JOHN: Because she keeps calling back.

JILL: Why would a wrong number keep calling back?

JOHN: She says my cat's in her garden.

JILL: You don't have a cat.

JOHN: I know that.

JILL: I'm going home.

JOHN: No, wait, wait, Jill, I swear it's the truth. Wait. Phoebe, will you tell Jill why you called, please?

PHOEBE: OK.

JOHN: Talk to her.

JILL: I don't want to talk to her.

JOHN: Talk to her. What have you got to lose?

JILL: *(Hesitating, then taking the phone.)* Hello?

PHOEBE: Hi, Jill.

JILL: Who is this?

PHOEBE: This is Phoebe. Listen, Jill, does Mrs. Murphy know you're there?

JILL: John told me he wasn't married.

JOHN: I'm not married. *(Taking the phone.)* Phoebe, just tell her about the cat, all right?

JILL: I don't sleep with married men.

PHOEBE: I don't blame you, Jill.

JOHN: PHOEBE, WILL YOU JUST TELL HER ABOUT THE DAMNED CAT?

PHOEBE: All right, all right. Boy, men get so hysterical when their cats run away, don't they, Jill?

JILL: Phoebe, I'm a little confused here.

PHOEBE: Men confuse me, too. I'd much rather have a cat, but I'm allergic.

JILL: So am I.

PHOEBE: Really? Then how can you sleep with John? Don't you sneeze while you're doing it?

JILL: There's no cat here.

PHOEBE: I know. She's in my garden. And she seems to be growing.

JILL: So John gives you the cat when a woman sleeps over, is that how it works?

PHOEBE: You mean he threw the cat out when he knew you were coming? Boy, is Mrs. Murphy gonna be pissed.

JILL: He says there is no Mrs. Murphy.

PHOEBE: Then who is that tall woman in the straw hat I see watering his flowers all the time?

JILL: John, you son of a bitch, you ARE married.

JOHN: *(Taking the phone.)* Phoebe, what the hell have you been telling her?

JILL: That does it. I'm putting my clothes on and getting out of here. Goodbye, Phoebe.

*(Jill slams down the phone and stomps off.)*

JOHN: Jill. Wait a minute. I can explain this. Well, some of it.

*(He goes after her. Phoebe redials. The phone rings. John returns after a bit, weary, and picks up the phone.)*

Hello, Phoebe. How are you?

PHOEBE: Is Jill all right? I think we got disconnected.

JOHN: Jill has locked herself in the bathroom with her clothes and turned on the shower.

PHOEBE: Gee, I hope she's not going to cut her throat or something.

JOHN: Sounds like a serious option to me, at this point.

PHOEBE: Well, you shouldn't be cheating on your wife like that.

JOHN: I'M NOT MARRIED.

PHOEBE: Then you shouldn't be cheating on that woman in the straw hat.

JOHN: Phoebe, I am not the person you think I am.

PHOEBE: Wait. There's something happening in the garden.

JOHN: What? My cat is eating your watermelons?

PHOEBE: Maybe that's not your cat after all.

JOHN: Oh, no, it's my cat, Phoebe. My cat loves watermelons.

PHOEBE: But this seems to be a lot bigger than a cat. This is a very large object moving in my garden.

JOHN: Maybe it's a bear.

PHOEBE: It could be a bear. I don't know. It seems —

JOHN: What? It's doing the tango, isn't it, Phoebe?

PHOEBE: No, but it seems to have — noticed me. John, there's this big, dark thing in my garden, and it's looking at this window. This is kind of scary. It's so dark out there, I can't see it real clearly, but it seems to be coming toward the house.

JOHN: Phoebe, are you on drugs?

PHOEBE: No, just valium, but it doesn't work on me. This is really spooky. This is pretty alarming. John, could you come over here?

JOHN: I don't know where you live, Phoebe.

PHOEBE: Yes you do. I live right next door.

JOHN: Nobody lives next door to me, Phoebe. There's woods on one side and an empty house on the other.

PHOEBE: It's not empty. It's my house.

JOHN: It isn't your house. Nobody lives there.

PHOEBE: John, this thing is up against the window. It's trying to look in the window at me. You've got to help me.

JOHN: Take it easy, Phoebe. Just tell me your address.

PHOEBE: It's right next to your address. John, it's banging against the window. It wants in my house.

JOHN: Just tell me your last name and I'll look your address up in the phone book.

PHOEBE: You know my last name.

*(Sound of glass shattering.)*

Oh, my God. It broke the glass. John, get over here right now. I mean it. Right now.

*(Blackout on Phoebe. Sound of the dial tone.)*

JOHN: Phoebe? Hello? Did you hang up? I'm talking to a dial tone here. *(John hangs up. Pause.)* Weird. Very weird. *(He waits. The phone rings. He picks it up.)* Hello? Phoebe? Hello? *(Silence from the other end.)* Phoebe? Talk to me. Hello? Is anybody there?

*(The light fades on him and goes out.)*

END OF PLAY

# Fog

## DON NIGRO

CHARACTERS

    RYE

    LEA

    ANN

SETTING

    A fog-shrouded woods

            •    •    •

*Lights up on a dimly lit stage, shadows of branches. Rye, sitting on the ground, and Lea and Ann, who sit together at a little distance from him. Darkness is all around them. Sense of woods in fog.*

RYE: Because of the fog. Because of the branches of trees clutching into the white like smoke devoured and all transformed. Because one's perception of depth is altered by desire. Because one is embraced by naked flesh. Because of her breasts. Because betrayal is. Because in the fog the birds grow silent. To walk through the fog is a dream.

LEA: Whisper to him. Watch him stumble through the woods. Fog wet on his clothing. Hands bloody, ripped by thorns, mud on his knees from where he has fallen. There is a hangman walking in this place.

ANN: I have lost something at Maidenhead. It is a squeaking bag of Renaissance grotesques. Come into the woods, says the voice. To touch her breasts. The nature of betrayal is uncertainty. Or certainty. And copulation. The end of love is always madness.

RYE: When the fog descends she is there in the woods. I can feel her now.

LEA: I caress him like branches of willow.

RYE: She is part of the fog. She is the substance in which I am lost.

LEA: I am the place he has come from, and where he is going.

RYE: I wander in the woods, stumbling over fallen trees.

LEA: The fog is a labyrinth you are lost in. Touch it.

RYE: I can hear her whispering because I remember her breasts.

LEA: When he touches my breasts I shudder. Under my breasts and the nipples of my breasts.

RYE: Because I remember her tears.

LEA: I am shuddering in the fog, in the mud, in the leaves. My beloved has strong, bloody hands.

RYE: Her passion, her cruelty.

LEA: He wanders deeper into the labyrinth of fog.

RYE: Because I have walked in the woods with her.

LEA: The fog devours him.

RYE: Because when the fog comes I hear her whispering and I must come to her.

LEA: He will strike his head on a branch and stumble, fall into the leaves. Embrace of the fog, damp clutching all in the brown and yellow leaves.

RYE: Because of the fog and because I have buried her somewhere here in the leaves.

ANN: No betrayal is imaginary. All betrayals are real, although some betrayals are not what you thought. When you look into the eyes of betrayal, what you see is the mirror image of your own unfaithfulness.

RYE: I am kissing her now. This did not happen. This is real. Her lips are real. I can feel her heart beating.

ANN: Why do we remember the past? Why don't we remember the future?

LEA: I can remember the future, she said, but I move inexorably toward the past. We were peeling potatoes together in the kitchen. He was watching us. Two red eyes glowing in the dark, like an animal in the woods.

ANN: I have lost something at Maidenhead.

LEA: Touch me. Touch me naked in the bath together. Listen.

ANN: I hear crows across an empty field.

LEA: Because he has buried me here in the leaves, crows will pick at his bones in the fog in the midst of the vast, dead labyrinth of woods which cannot.

ANN: Betrayal starts before you think it does. It never ends. Or perhaps it has no beginning, perhaps it was always built into the nature of things. Perhaps it is what we can't quite remember when we are children, the echo of ancient betrayals waiting to happen.

RYE: What physical acts were performed there?

ANN: Mirrors, fog, woods and naked flesh in bedrooms. We three like figures in a dream. A squeaking bag of Renaissance grotesques.

LEA: Whose dream? His, mine, or yours?

ANN: You loved me first.

RYE: Yes.

ANN: I allowed you to take certain liberties with my person.

RYE: Yes.

ANN: You lay above me in the woods, very still, fully clothed, in the autumn, your heart pounding.

RYE: Yes.

ANN: I could feel you between my legs.

RYE: Yes.

ANN: Kissing. Lips together. But no more.

RYE: It's very cold here.

ANN: And in the abandoned church.

RYE: Yes.

ANN: I let you hold me in the afternoon. I let you kiss me, and press yourself against me, and put your hand there. But nothing more.

RYE: Yes.

ANN: And then one night I lay in your bed with you.

RYE: Yes.

ANN: But I would not let you hold me. Warmth of our bodies, nearly naked, side by side, trembling, hearts pounding, until I fell asleep.

LEA: It's very cold in the woods. There is a hangman walking in these woods.

ANN: And when I awoke in the morning, your hand was caressing my breast, and there between my legs, and I lay trembling, eyes closed, until I had almost given in, and you could tell I had almost given in, and then I sat up and walked into the kitchen, and you knelt there naked and grieving on the bed, like one of those God has forgotten. I'm taking a shower, I said.

RYE: Yes.

ANN: I stood under the shower with my eyes closed, and heard you step into the shower. I felt your naked flesh against mine. I felt your hands on my flesh.

RYE: Yes.

ANN: And then I told you.

RYE: Yes.

ANN: I told you I wanted to kiss her.

LEA: Yes.

ANN: And you held me naked in the shower until the water was very cold.

LEA: There are many crows in this place.

ANN: I made you swear that you would help me. You swore that you would help me. Because I was afraid. You swore.

RYE: Yes.

LEA: You brought me to your house one night. We drank tea and then I let you take me to bed. We made love for hours with the light on, desperate, clutching, moaning together like two animals, thrusting and wet, and sweat and desperation. Then you pulled the blanket over our two naked bodies, and turned out the light, and held me very tenderly, and we slept.

ANN: Two red eyes, watching in the darkness.

LEA: And in the morning there were dandelions.

RYE: Which cannot. Which cannot be. Which has no source in.

ANN: You didn't speak to her of me.

RYE: No.

ANN: You didn't speak to her of me. You swore to me you would, but instead you slept with her, and you didn't speak to her of me.

RYE: Yes.

ANN: I was angry.

RYE: You were angry.

ANN: I was very, very angry. And I said horrible things to you.

RYE: Yes.

ANN: And I told you I could never love you, only her.

RYE: Yes.

LEA: I waited for him to call. All I could think of was that night, flesh straining together, hearts pounding, copulation copulation copulation, entering me like night again and into me like death.

RYE: Which is not, which cannot be, which can be only something I imagine, which is a nightmare in which. Betrayal is.

LEA: And when he didn't call, and didn't call, I went to his house, but he wasn't there. I went to the graveyard, where he walked at night, but he wasn't there.

ANN: I trusted him, to speak to her, because he loved me, and because I was afraid, and he betrayed me. I have lost something at Maidenhead. Do you hear the voices? There are many crows in this place.

LEA: Then I went to the woods. It was morning now, and the fog had crept into everything, there was nothing that morning that was not fog. I found him by the woods, looking at his hands. I put my hands in his and told him to come into the woods. Come into the woods, I said. Make love to me.

ANN: Make love to me. I want you to make love to me.

LEA: He took me deep into the woods and he made love to me in the fog, in the woods, deep into the woods, he made love to me, but he was angry, he made love to me but he was angry, it was frightening and exciting, his anger, his passion, the violence of his despair. It was the ecstasy of grief, and he was lost, and I was lost. And then he strangled me in the woods. And he buried me in the leaves.

ANN: That which is not, nevertheless, remains because.

LEA: Having wandered too far in now to go back, all that remains is haunting.

RYE: Into the twisted branches.

ANN: To know that one has been betrayed.

LEA: Come into the woods. Into the twisted branches. Something lost.

ANN: Not knowing the exact moment of one's betrayal, but knowing that the moment exists in time, perhaps in the past, probably in the present, and certainly in the future, and, most terrible of all, that one has written the play one's self, from out of one's own fear and desperation.

LEA: Can't see, can't understand, everything darkness, his hands around my throat. Come into the woods. This has not happened yet.

RYE: Come into the woods, she said. I have something to show you. My throat is constricted. I can't swallow. There is fog in my lungs. I take off my belt and hang myself from a tree limb in the woods.

LEA: When the sun burns the fog off the rooftops of the village he will dangle there in the twisted branches and crows will pick out his eyes.

ANN: I have lost something at Maidenhead. It is a squeaking bag of Renaissance grotesques. Come into the woods, says the voice. To touch her breasts. The nature of betrayal is uncertainty. Or certainty. And copulation. The end of love is always madness.

RYE: To touch her breasts.

ANN: I have lost something at Maidenhead. In men there is always darkness. A woman is fog and woods. At night they are in my head forever, the voices. Here in the cell of my autumn desperation, they will not let me use my hands. There are many crows in this place. They run about and flap their arms at me. A squeaking bag of Renaissance grotesques. The nature of time is memory. The nature of memory is betrayal. The nature of betrayal. The nature of betrayal. Is fog.

*(The light fades on them and goes out.)*

END OF PLAY

# The Concorde Fallacy

## DOUG RAND

*for Dafna*

*The Concorde Fallacy* was first staged in February 2005 by Florida
   Community College at Jacksonville (FCCJ) DramaWorks. This
evening of reader's theater revolved around the theme of dating, and
also included *Check, Please* by Jonathan Rand and *Reservations* by Lisa
Rand. ("The Rand Tour," they called it.) Ian Mairs directed the following cast: David — Herb Green; Julie — Catie Fry; Veronica —
   Summer Deckert.

CHARACTERS
DAVID
JULIE
VERONICA

SETTING
Could be anywhere

•   •   •

*First date: David and Julie are out somewhere.*

DAVID: So.

JULIE: So.

DAVID: So you own a restaurant? I was so amazed when I saw that. I think that deep down, everyone wants to quit their job and open a restaurant.

JULIE: I *used* to own a restaurant. Actually just a coffee shop. We didn't have a liquor license or anything — no need to be too impressed.

DAVID: What happened? Was your coffee shop vanquished by the Starbucks Deathstar?

JULIE: You'd think, but no. It was really an Old Economy problem — my place was very pen-and-paper, very DOS-era. The whole place was centered around dating, actually, with big books of personals you could flip through, and it worked really well for a while. But then came the Internet, and — as we know — that's where all the cool kids are meeting these days.

DAVID: That and speed dating.

JULIE: You've never descended to that, have you?

DAVID: Just once. It was very stressful.

JULIE: I would imagine so. No depth.

*(The conversation lapses for a beat.)*

DAVID: So. What do you do now?

JULIE: I'm a consultant.

DAVID: I've never had a clue what that means.

JULIE: It generally means someone to whom you pay a lot of money to tell you exactly what you want to hear. But I'm not that kind of consultant. I'm a dating coach.

DAVID: For real?

JULIE: Yes. I sort of invented the position.

DAVID: So dating is like a sport, huh?

JULIE: Plenty would say so, sure, but most of my clients aren't in that competitive a mode. I see myself less like a football coach, and more like a vocal coach or an acting coach.

DAVID: So dating isn't a game, it's an audition.

JULIE: Sure.

DAVID: Am I passing?

*(Instant shift. First debrief.)*

VERONICA: What's the expert opinion?

JULIE: It went fine.

VERONICA: Really?

JULIE: Sure.

VERONICA: That, then, is the end of that.

JULIE: What?

VERONICA: It's over! Next up! He shall some day recover!

JULIE: I said it went fine.

VERONICA: Fine is for losers. Fine means Not Good.

JULIE: It wasn't Not Good, it just was Not Thrilling.

VERONICA: Explicate.

JULIE: I don't have to tell you . . .

VERONICA: Yet tell you must. Why else am I before you?

JULIE: It was a perfectly serviceable first date — decent conversation, the shadow of an attraction, and no huge screaming red flags.

VERONICA: A perfect recipe for moving on, immediately.

JULIE: You obviously don't know my Rule of Dating #1: First impressions can be deceiving, so a second date is always worth a shot.

VERONICA: I would advise you to step lively on over to my Rule of Dating #2: To whit: Rule #1 is for people with far too much time on their hands.

JULIE: I certainly have time to give a perfectly nice person the benefit of the doubt.

VERONICA: What, may I ask, are you seeking in this perfectly nice person? Are you dating in order to find a soul mate? To shut your parents up? To get hitched? Rich? Laid? What precisely do you want from this carnival of awkwardness?

JULIE: I'll go with soul mate.

VERONICA: Excellent! An arguably concrete goal! Now we're cooking with grease.

JULIE: That we are.

VERONICA: Do you want to have children with this soul mate?

JULIE: Yes.

VERONICA: Do you want to have healthy children?

JULIE: Yes.

VERONICA: Do you want these healthy children to spring forth natural and goopy from your own plumbing, or do you want to go mail-order?

JULIE: I'd prefer the former.

VERONICA: Very well: If you want to produce healthy children, you must do so by the age of thirty-five — some would say thirty-three to be on the very safe side — and that means it is imperative that you be married by thirty if you want to spend any quality time with your husband before the wee ones utterly consume your lives — therefore marriage by thirty is absolutely mandatory, and when we factor in sufficient time for engagement and courtship, this means that if by twenty-seven you haven't met The One, you'd better run.

JULIE: There's no such thing as The One.

VERONICA: Are you seeing A One, at least?

JULIE: I don't know yet. I believe in evolution, not the Big Bang.

*(Instant shift. Second date.)*

DAVID: I really don't mean for this to come out the wrong way, but —

JULIE: What?

DAVID: Are you really a dating coach?

JULIE: Why would I lie about something like that? Are *you* really a chef?

DAVID: Yes, and also no, I'm technically a pastry chef — I just meant, for someone who coaches people on dating for a living, you seem really nervous.

JULIE: Ah.

DAVID: I mean, I'm nervous too, I just —

JULIE: No, don't apologize. I am nervous — congrats on that — I'm actually not the best on dates. It's kind of impossible to coach yourself — but, here's the thing: I'm really very good at what I do.

DAVID: I didn't mean to suggest that you weren't —

JULIE: Don't apologize, just trust me: I invented this job, I pioneered the field, and I'm really extremely good. Like statistically significant good. Ninety-six percent of my clients get asked out a second time. Fifty-three percent have gone on to serious long-term relationships — trust me, 53 percent is a phenomenal success rate — and there are 127 couples in this city who wouldn't be married now without me.

DAVID: OK.

JULIE: Uh-huh.

DAVID: I believe you.

JULIE: Here's the thing: When you were a kid, did you read all those Encyclopedia Brown mysteries?

DAVID: Yeah! Man, I haven't thought about those books in —

JULIE: Do you remember the one about the town with two barbers?

DAVID: That's not a joke?

JULIE: No, it's the world's greatest allegory for what I do, and for any weirdness you're experiencing this afternoon: Encyclopedia Brown's town has only two barbers — one with a great haircut, and one with a terrible haircut. And Encyclopedia always chooses to get his hair cut by the barber with a mess on his head. Why?

DAVID: Why?

JULIE: Why.

DAVID: I have no idea.

JULIE: Because: It's really hard to cut your own hair.

DAVID: So the barber with the good haircut must be responsible for the other guy's bad haircut . . .

JULIE: And vice versa.

DAVID: I got it.

JULIE: As far as I know, our town has only two dating coaches.

*(Second debrief.)*

JULIE: See, I'd really prefer it if you just told me to sit up straight and make eye contact.

VERONICA: To be successful at dating, you must first ground yourself in a coherent intellectual framework.

JULIE: No, to be successful at dating, you must avoid ordering corn on the cob.

VERONICA: You, my dear, are a former barista, while I am a certified actuary with two Ph.D.'s.

JULIE: Fine, enlighten me.

VERONICA: Lesson #1 for Soul-Mate Seekers: Destiny is nonsense. Fate is a hoax for callow little children, as are Kismet, the Intended, the One —

JULIE: The Bashert.

VERONICA: The bawhat?

JULIE: It's Yiddish for the same idea. God slices one soul into a boy half and a girl half, then sends them out of two wombs to go find and complete one another.

VERONICA: I think that was in *Hedwig*.

JULIE: Yes it was.

VERONICA: Very well: Eradicate such refuse from your mind entirely. There are six billion people on this planet, and you can reasonably expect to meet only a scant few thousand of them in your lifetime — perhaps five thousand, maximum, and then only if you are very persistent with Friendster. Even if there were one half of your cleft soul walking around longing for you, there is less than one chance in 26.3 million that you will actually meet this person, given that they are probably milking goats in Upper Volta. There are no prefabricated matches, only varying degrees of attraction and revulsion. Since the clock is ever ticking, it behooves you to stack the deck in your favor. Thus: Forget about bars; bars are a random trawl, too much worthless bycatch, possibly skewed toward alcoholics. Let your priorities guide you. If you can't imagine living with someone who doesn't appreciate art, then pick up men in a museum. If you must have someone who can cook, join an epicurean club. If there isn't one near you, start one. This is not devious; this is obvious.

JULIE: I already did those things. Now I'm dating a pastry chef.

VERONICA: Now you are "dating"? As in, you wish to go on yet another date with this nonstarter?

JULIE: I'm hedging my bets. You should appreciate that.

*(Third date.)*

DAVID: So your dating coach is the bad barber?

JULIE: I'd like to think so, but really we're just very different in our approach. I'm all tactics, and she's all strategy. She's the von Clausewitz of dating, and I'm more of a God-is-in-the-details, practical kind of trainer. I teach my clients how to write their online blurbs — (it's a new art form, believe me [well-done by the way]) — and then we move on to how to choose a restaurant, conversational topics to avoid, basic etiquette, things like that.

DAVID: I'm really sorry again that I was late tonight.

JULIE: It's fine. But if you were my client, for example, you'd know valuable dating principles like Don't Ever Keep a Girl Waiting, and For God's Sake Don't Ask to Finish Her Uneaten Portion, and also Three Dates Without Making a Move Makes a Girl Wonder What the Hell.

DAVID: I'm really sorry if I was rude, and —

JULIE: The fact that I'm still sitting here means you should be thinking about how to apply that last principle.

*(Beat.)*

DAVID: My ex's first husband wrote his doctoral thesis on Clausewitz.

JULIE: You want to talk about that?

DAVID: The thesis?

JULIE: No, your Ex Files.

DAVID: Is this the time or the place?

JULIE: Relax, I'm a professional. Lay it on me.

DAVID: OK, but there's not much to tell, really. I met my ex a few years after her divorce, we were together for four and a half years, thought about living together, got spooked — mutually — and I haven't heard hide or hair of her in the six months since then.

JULIE: Six months?

DAVID: I don't have any baggage.

JULIE: OK.

*(Third debrief.)*

VERONICA: One must *NEVER SAY* "I don't have any baggage"! One must never believe a person when they say it! It is one of many all-too-telling declarations that is always and forever a bald-faced, delusional lie. Here is another: "I'm not a racist." And another: "I have a really great sense of humor." True virtue abhors self-advertisement. Only psychopaths lack baggage.

JULIE: I hate theory.

VERONICA: Theory is essential! Theory is victory! And my theories brim with insight:

*(Counting off on her fingers:)*

Cast a wide net with a fine grain.

Never waste time.

Love is not blind, so go to the gym for God's sake.

And also:

Instinct is not a myth.

JULIE: What are you saying, Veronica?

VERONICA: I believe only that we know what we know when we know it.

JULIE: I am not hearing this from you of all people. I refuse to be infected by The Poet's Imperative!

VERONICA: Do I hear a *theory* coming on, my dear?

JULIE: The Poet's Imperative is not a theory — it's a conspiracy! It's a dangerous virus that was weaponized by Shakespeare and contaminates millions of people through pop songs. It says that love will knock you over in one little instant, and if you're still standing then it can't be love. It says never be satisfied by anything less than fireworks and fevers. It says your quiet love is nothing. It says the world's greatest romance was born in one moment, when Romeo saw Juliet across a crowded room. Do you know how much damage has been done single-handedly by "Some Enchanted Evening"?

VERONICA: Your problems are not the direct result of *South Pacific*.

JULIE: All I'm saying is that love takes time.

VERONICA: We are agreed. How much time do you think you have left?

*(Fourth or so date.)*

JULIE: You need to level with me.

DAVID: Is this our RDT?

JULIE: For your information, the Relationship-Defining Talk is for the sooner of the sixth date or the first sexual experience — in my professional opinion, we've got a ways to go.

DAVID: What's wrong?

JULIE: I've read every Encyclopedia Brown story. I can't believe it took me this long to figure it out.

DAVID: Julie . . .

JULIE: Did you just say my *name?* People don't say other people's names, *David,* unless they're pissed off, guilty as sin, or climaxing.

DAVID: I never thought of that. Hey — you're absolutely right.

JULIE: You said that your ex had a first husband, that you met her after their divorce, and that you haven't heard anything about her since you split up six months ago.

DAVID: That's all true.

JULIE: But! You wouldn't say "first husband" unless there were a second one. You'd say "ex-husband." How do you know she got married again?

DAVID: I remember that Encyclopedia Brown story you're talking about! I can't believe it's relevant to the real world.

JULIE: Shut up and confess.

DAVID: OK. I lied about not being in touch with my ex anymore.

JULIE: Were you married?

DAVID: No.

JULIE: *Are* you married?

DAVID: No. I swear. I must have said "first husband" because somewhere along the line, I started thinking of myself as the inevitable second. But we did break up.

JULIE: Don't keep lying to me.

DAVID: We really did. It's just that it was . . . provisional.

JULIE: Don't say it . . .

DAVID: We wanted to see other people.

JULIE: "Before you got serious."

DAVID: Right.

JULIE: Right.

DAVID: I really like you.

JULIE: That's very nice. But nooooooooo-ho-ho *no* RDT for you tonight.

DAVID: I'm not on the rebound.

JULIE: I *wish* you were on the rebound; that would be a relative honor. But apparently I'm an experimental wild-oats repository.

DAVID: Listen, Julie — sorry, I won't say your name again, just listen: Something always told me that what I had with my ex wasn't It. You know what I mean, right? You must see this all the time. You watch all these people getting married just because they feel like they've already invested too much to pull out, but that's crazy, that's irrational, and the Real Deal should be so clear that it eliminates all doubt, right? Isn't that what's worth waiting for? Isn't just fine not enough?

*(Last words, into the ether.)*

JULIE: This is the Tale of the Concorde, which lends itself to all manner of allegories: Once upon a time the British and the French, experiencing a rush of unlikely bonhomie, hooked up to make a supersonic plane. They drew up plans and made huge investments and got down to work. Soon they were straining the budget, though, and then they were way over-budget, and then, one day, they were so far overbudget that *there was no way the plane could ever make back all the money they'd already put into it.* The rational choice was to give up, cut bait, and pull out. But instead they said, "Well, we've come this far." As so many do. And thus the Concorde was born, never to make its investors a penny. And some think it was a colossal waste, but others think it was a beautiful plane while it lasted.

VERONICA: Every man is a Peter Pan, unwilling to grow up, and every woman is a Captain Hook, murderous-furious at Peter and always pursued by a tick-tocking crocodile. The biological clock winds its spring backwards through time, sinking its hooks into your heart and hurtling you into the all-too-foreseeable future. Men, with their sperm everlasting, have no such clock-in-the-croc. Do not be bamboozled by their contemptible confidence as they patiently wait for The One. They can afford to do so. You cannot. You must never compromise now, or sooner or later, you will be forced to.

DAVID: So.

JULIE: So.

DAVID: I want you to know that I can be in this for the long haul, Julie. I mean that. If you need more time, I can wait. I can take it slow. I mean, where's the fire, right?

JULIE: Yeah, where's the fire.

END OF PLAY

# Knots

Lisa Soland

CHARACTERS
> OLDER WOMAN: a middle-aged woman — Karen, many years later
> KAREN: college student, about twenty
> DOUG: college student, about twenty

SETTING
> Doug's childhood bedroom in his parents' home in West Palm Beach, Florida

TIME
> Today

• • •

*SETTING: Doug's bedroom, which consists mainly of a twin-sized bed. AT RISE: Doug and Karen are sitting on the bed. Older Woman addresses the audience.*

OLDER WOMAN: *(To audience.)* I dated this guy in college, kind of a codependent type, you know. Always telling you he loved you. But he had a car, which was great, 'cause we got to go places. One time, we were visiting his folks in West Palm during spring break and we're in his bedroom from when he was a kid, sitting on the bed, and he tells me . . .

DOUG: *(To Karen.)* I love you more than anything in the world.

OLDER WOMAN: And I'm thinkin', "Crap. I hope he doesn't expect me to tell him that back because . . . I don't. In fact, I can think of a ton of things I love better than him . . . like *me*, for instance." Anyway, he says it, just the same.

DOUG: *(To Karen, repeating just as before.)* I love you more than anything in the world.

OLDER WOMAN: And I'm sitting there looking at him. Just looking at him. It's a lot of pressure, you know. Sitting there in the room he grew up in, on the bed he grew up on, with his parents and everyone running around the house. So I thought I'd better smile and say . . . something.

KAREN: *(She smiles.)* Oh, that's so nice to say. Wow, thanks honey. Thank you. Thanks a lot.
*(She pats his hand.)*

OLDER WOMAN: And then it comes. The guilt trip. Subtle at first and then the ol' freakin' guilt trip.

DOUG: What? Don't you feel that way too?

KAREN: What way?

DOUG: What I just said.

KAREN: What?

DOUG: You heard me.

OLDER WOMAN: *(To Doug, though he doesn't hear her.)* Yes, she did. But it gives her time to think if you repeat yourself. So please, just patiently repeat yourself.

DOUG: *(Patiently.)* I said that I loved you more than anything else in the world.

OLDER WOMAN: Good boy. *(Then turning to Karen.)* Thinking. Thinking.

KAREN: OK. OK. And I said, "Thanks." Thanks.

DOUG: You don't feel the same way.

KAREN: Well, I don't think I would word it quite like that.

DOUG: You don't love me.

KAREN: No, no that's not it. I do love you.

DOUG: Then why don't you say it?

*(She does.)*

KAREN: I love you.

DOUG: No, you don't.

KAREN: Yes, I do. I love you, Doug. I love you.

DOUG: No . . . *(To himself.)* What is it? I'm picking up on something but I can't quite put my finger on it.

KAREN: Put your finger on what?

DOUG: You. I can't put my finger on you.

KAREN: OK.

DOUG: You may love me but it's not quite the same.

KAREN: Not quite the same as what?

DOUG: As me. As me, Karen. You don't love me like I love you.

KAREN: OK.

DOUG: Why do you keep saying that – "OK," like that? What's that supposed to mean?

KAREN: It means OK. That's all. It means OK.

DOUG: *(Realizing.)* You don't love me like I love you. That's what it is!

KAREN: Well, how exactly do you love me that's so different?

DOUG: I love you more than anything in the world, Karen. That's how I love you that's so different.

KAREN: But what exactly does that mean?

DOUG: What do you mean, what does it mean? It means what it means.

It means there's nothing I love more. I don't love skiing more than you, reading great literature more than you, food, lobster more than you, uhm . . . All my favorite things. The beach. The sun. Margaritas. Jimmy Buffet. Nothing. Nothing more than you. Not my parents, not my brother, not my dog. Nothing. You are it.

KAREN: Not your dog?

DOUG: Nothing more than you.

KAREN: Really?

DOUG: Can you say that, Karen? Can you say that you feel that way about me?

*(Pause.)*

KAREN: I don't have a dog.

DOUG: *(He closes his eyes, so angry and so hurt.)* Can you say that about me?

KAREN: No. No, I can't.

DOUG: No! No?!!! Why not?

KAREN: I don't know. I just can't.

DOUG: Well, that's just great. That's just great. Thanks a lot. Thanks a lot, Karen. What am I supposed to do now? What am I supposed to do now, huh?!!!

OLDER WOMAN: Oh, throw a fit. You always did.

KAREN: I don't know.

OLDER WOMAN: Throw a fit until I tie myself into a knot.

DOUG: *(Throwing a fit.)* I don't understand why you just can't say it. Why can't you just fucking say it, Karen? Is it so hard to say something, anything, even if it's not exactly what you mean? What the hell is your fucking problem, anyway? Did your parents raise you so fucking straight that you can never, ever say anything slightly different than what you really, truly, deeply in your heart, mean? Huh?!!! What's wrong with you?!!!

OLDER WOMAN: *(Simply.)* She can't say it 'cause it ain't true.

KAREN: *(Sweetly.)* You want me to lie?

DOUG: No, I don't want you to lie.

OLDER WOMAN: He wants you to lie.

DOUG: I want you to feel the same way I do.

OLDER WOMAN: *(To audience.)* Saying, "OK" gave me time to think. That's why I said it — to give myself time to think. It's a great word, "OK." It's like talking about the weather but you don't have to talk about the weather you just say OK instead. So I said it . . .

KAREN: OK.

OLDER WOMAN: . . . which gave me a good five seconds more to think.

*(Beat.)*

And then he said it.

DOUG: *(Lost, he throws up his arms, sarcastic.)* "OK."

OLDER WOMAN: And then added the word . . .

DOUG: Great.

OLDER WOMAN: . . . which bought me another five or six seconds.

*(Beat.)*

And in that time I thought, "Jeez, I'm stuck down here in West Palm and there ain't no way I'm getting back up to Tallahassee on my own so I better try to figure out how to get myself out of this . . . gracefully."

KAREN: *(Very convincing.)* Listen, Doug. I love you. I love you. Just because I can't say it the same way you can, using the same words you do, doesn't mean that my words mean any less. Love is love. It's love, honey. I love you.

OLDER WOMAN: Oh my God.

*(To Karen.)* You love the fact that he has a car and that you don't have any money and that you don't "love" walking five hundred miles to get back to where you need to be so you can be yourself — alone, free. Remember that? Remember YOURSELF? Remember what that feels like to be honest and free and not have to lie? Not have to change yourself to make something work? Not have to tie yourself up into knots like one of those fattening, salty pretzels you buy at the mall when you've hit middle age? Knots, Karen. Remember knots?

*(Beat.)*

Be clear. At least in your own head, please be clear about what it is you love.

*(Whispering in Karen's ear.)*

His car. You love his car.

KAREN: *(To Doug, ignoring Older Woman.)* I love *you*. OK.

*(Taking his hand.)*

I love you, honey.

DOUG: All right. I'm sorry.

KAREN: It's OK.

OLDER WOMAN: *(Nodding.)* Knots.

*(Fade out.)*


END OF PLAY

# Lucky

ROSANNA STAFFA

*Lucky* was presented by Thirst Theater (founded by
Alan Berks, Chris Carlson, and Tracey Maloney) at Joe's
Garage in Minneapolis. The actors were: Sam — Charles
Frazer; Rod — Bob Davis; Waitress — Sonja Parks.

CHARACTERS

    SAM

    ROD

    A WAITRESS

SETTING

    A coffee shop

• • •

*Sam and Rod in a coffee shop. They read the menus, the waitress takes out pencil and note pad*

ROD: *(Looks around.)* Nice place. I need a good place to end this forsaken day, a velvet glove to slide into.
*(Points with his thumb.)*
Young waitress, nice ass.
*(To Sam.)* Call her.

SAM: Waitress.
*(The Waitress approaches.)*

ROD: *(To Sam.)* She came. Send her away.

SAM: Away . . . where?

ROD: Anywhere. For bread.

SAM: Waitress? Bread, please.

WAITRESS: Bread?

ROD: Yes, bread. *(To Sam.)* Watch: Now she goes away.
*(Rod checks out the waitress' body while she goes to get the bread.)*

ROD: She went. Now she's coming back. Like-a-kite-on-a-string.
*(The waitress comes back with a basket of bread.)*

ROD: Here she comes!

WAITRESS: Bread is the host of visiting spirits, they become one with the people eating it.
*(Puts the bread on the table.)*

SAM: *(Looks in the basket.)* There're pieces? No crackers?

WAITRESS: No.

ROD: *(Short.)* It's fine.
*(To Sam.)*
Tell her something. She's standing here listening.

SAM: What shall I say?

ROD: Talk to her.

*(A little silence. Sam looks up then down, quickly.)*

SAM: Coffee please.

ROD: Make it two.

SAM: Thank you.

*(The waitress goes.)*

ROD: Don't be silly, you can tell her all you want, she listens to anything. Why didn't you think of something to tell her?

SAM: I did, a bit.

ROD: Oh, yeah?

SAM: *(Nods.)* Then I noticed she had tiny bones and kind of lost my thought. My heart started pumping fast. I saw ventricles, arteries, all alone, fast at work, racing past the Big Dipper.

ROD: Alright, tell her that. She'll stand there, shift a bit. I like it when they stand and shift. That's when they really like what you're saying. If she smiles, she doesn't like it. If we don't order enough, she'll stop coming by. No food no talk.

SAM: *(Rehearses.)* I noticed you have tiny bones.

ROD: What else?

SAM: I haven't noticed anything else.

ROD: The Big Dipper stuff, tell her that.

SAM: *(Nervous.)* I need water first.

ROD: Water!

*(The waitress approaches with coffee.)*

ROD: We are having a good talk, my friend and I. He wants to tell you about your bones.

WAITRESS: What about my bones?

ROD: *(To Sam.)* Tell her.

*(To the Waitress.)*

A thought about your bones raced through his mind, got him all discombobulated.

WAITRESS: Really? That's psychic, he's psychic.

ROD: Who?!

WAITRESS: Your friend.

ROD: Ah, yeah.

WAITRESS: I've got finger arthritis, it's awful. Your friend doesn't look like a doctor . . . so he's psychic!

SAM: You have arthritis? In your fingers?

WAITRESS: When I wake up . . . they're like THIS . . . craaamped.

SAM: Aspirin, you can take aspirin.

ROD: Hey! Where's the water?

SAM: I read it someplace: When you lose hope, you get arthritis, it's automatic.

ROD: *(Raises his eyes to the ceiling.)* Jesus.

SAM: It's a matter of hope.

WAITRESS: Hope was a cruelty of Zeus, who put it in Pandora's box so people
would put up with all the other shit he'd put in the box.
*(The Waitress goes.)*

ROD: What did you talk about arthritis for? It's fucking depressing.

SAM: What did she lose hope about?

ROD: We're having FUN and you go talk about ARTHRITIS. All I see is her
fucking arthritis now.

SAM: She should at least TRY aspirin.

ROD: A crack in the conversation, this small, and she slides right in with her
arthritis.
*(Drums his fingers on the table.)*
Give me a break. *Give me a break.*
*(To Sam.)*
Stop looking around. What are you looking around for? I don't want her
here.

SAM: I'm thirsty.

ROD: *(Calls out.)* Water.

WAITRESS: Water, two.

ROD: Three.

WAITRESS: Why?

ROD: Just in case.
*(To Sam.)*
I don't want her back and forth, back and forth with her arthritis.
*(The waitress brings coffee and water, two glasses.)*

WAITRESS: Maybe I'll try aspirin, good advice.

SAM: Oh, it's nothing . . .
*(Quotes.)*
My heart is warm with the friends I make,
And better friends I'll not be knowing . . .

ROD: Oh, shut up.

SAM: A . . . poem . . .
*(The waitress shifts her weight, awkward.)*

WAITRESS: I always wanted to learn a poem.

SAM: I don't understand.

WAITRESS: I would like to learn a poem, short.

ROD: What the hell is going on here?

SAM: *(To the Waitress.)* Later. You better go. We need to talk alone, me and my friend.

WAITRESS: Real short is fine.

ROD: *(Pockets the bread.)* Give her the forsaken poem.

SAM: *(Hurried.)* How about this?

*(Quotes.)*

I said to heart, "How it goes?" Heart

Replied:

"Right as a Ribstone Pippin!" But it

lied

ROD: It's perfect

*(To the Waitress.)*

You got your poem.

WAITRESS: *(Repeats.)* . . . but it lied

*(To Sam.)*

It's sad. Isn't it?

*(Rod starts to say something, visibly agitated.)*

SAM: *(More hurried.)* Love, good night!

Must thou go

When the day

And the light

Need thee so?

*(The Waitress hands Sam a dollar.)*

WAITRESS: Here . . . Buy yourself some fruit . . . it's good for the skin, the brain too. They put Einstein's brain on ice, to study it. It's full of vitamins you bet.

ROD: OK OK. *La quenta!*

*(The Waitress does not give the check.)*

WAITRESS: This one is on me.

*(To Rod.)*

Your friend is really nice.

ROD: Now she'll tell you you look just like her brother.

WAITRESS: He doesn't look like my brother.

ROD: I didn't say he does.

WAITRESS: I'm not going to say he looks like my brother if he doesn't look like my brother.

ROD: Sure you would.

WAITRESS: What would I say THAT for?

ROD: *(Pointing at Sam.)* Because you like him, he's nice.

SAM: *(To Rod, fast.)* The coffee.

ROD: WHAT?

SAM: . . . It's getting cold maybe . . .

ROD: *It's perfectly fine.*

> *(To the Waitress.)*
>
> You like him take him, cut the bullshit, all you do all day is bullshit with your customers I know every word you say. Cut the bullshit and take him to be, be my guest. He might fuck like your brother.

WAITRESS: What the Hell.

> *(The Waitress throws a glass of water at Rod. Rod jumps up.)*

ROD: *(Advances toward the Waitress.)* I could call you something: fallen woman, trash, slut, whore, sodomite. Names. I won't, I believe in the survival of the soul.

> *(Sam restrains Rod.)*

SAM: *(To Rod.)* Rod, it's nothing, let's go.

> *(Rod laughs, conciliatory. Sam releases him.)*

ROD: Me? Hit a woman? ME?

> *(Rod springs around, punches Sam.)*

ROD: Goddam idiot.

WAITRESS: Stop it, I'm calling the manager.

> *(Rod punches Sam again. The Waitress runs off to call the manager.)*

ROD: Pimp, leper: a woman looks at you, you ditch me. LOOK at you. She sucked your brain bone dry, chewed, lapped it up, turned it into excrement.

SAM: Rod . . . what are you saying . . . Rod . . .

ROD: Don't you dare. Don't you dare stand up against me, ever.

> *(Starts going.)*
>
> I gave you everything, I saved your damn life, basically. WE'RE THROUGH.

> *(Rod runs out, Sam runs after him, calling him.)*

END OF PLAY

# Epiphany

## FREDERICK STROPPEL

*Epiphany* was first produced by the Theatre Artists Workshop of Westport in Norwalk, Connecticut, in July 2005, as part of their annual Word of the Week Festival. It was directed by Joanne Parady and had the following cast: Gaspar — David Rogers; Balthazar — Clayton Wheat; Melchior — Richard Leonard.

CHARACTERS
  GASPAR
  BALTHAZAR
  MELCHIOR

SETTING
  Bethlehem

• • •

*The little town of Bethlehem. Gaspar and Balthazar enter, in a state of rapture.*

GASPAR: We have seen him!

BALTHAZAR: We have seen the Child!

GASPAR: We have seen the manger where he was born, and stood in his blessed presence!

BALTHAZAR: We have bathed in his heavenly light!

GASPAR: We have borne witness to his wonder, praise the great almighty Lord!

BALTHAZAR: Amen, amen, amen!

*(They take a long, beatific sigh.)*

GASPAR: So — what do you want to do now?

BALTHAZAR: We could get a drink somewhere. I think I saw a bar on the way in.

GASPAR: I didn't eat. I'd like to maybe grab a falafel or something.

*(As they talk, Melchior enters, looking a bit troubled.)*

BALTHAZAR: Although — we should probably spread the word about the newborn King.

GASPAR: Yeah, I guess we should.

BALTHAZAR: People are gonna want to know about the Messiah showing up. That's big news.

GASPAR: *(Shrugs.)* Hey — they've waited five thousand years, what's a few hours more?

BALTHAZAR: That's a good point. Once we break this story, we're not gonna have a moment's peace. We should enjoy this last silent night.

GASPAR: Exactly.

BALTHAZAR: What do you say, Melchior — one drink for the road?

MELCHIOR: *(Uneasy.)* Uhh . . . No, I gotta get back home. Those camels are rented.

GASPAR: Something bothering you, Mel?

BALTHAZAR: Yes, you seem a bit subdued after such a momentous life-changing *zeitgeist* sort of event.

MELCHIOR: *(Uneasy.)* Well . . . Ya know, fellas, I gotta confess — this whole Messiah thing . . . ?

BALTHAZAR: Yes?

MELCHIOR: I don't know . . . To be honest, he looked like an ordinary little kid to me.

*(Balthazar and Gaspar are shocked.)*

GASPAR: An ordinary little kid?

BALTHAZAR: How can you say that? Did you see the light in his eyes, the mildness of his smile?

GASPAR: Did you see that halo above his head, that outshone the very stars?

MELCHIOR: *(Unimpressed.)* Did you see him pee on my robe when I picked him up?

BALTHAZAR: That but proves the divine mystery — he is both God *and* man.

MELCHIOR: Yeah, right. Where were all the angels and heavenly choirs they promised us? Where were the trumpets? Nothing! One measly shepherd playing a drum.

GASPAR: That kid was damn good. Why, he even had the ox and lamb keeping time.

BALTHAZAR: That's the whole point, Mel — the Lord reveals himself not in grand pronouncements, but in the simple truth of a shepherd's music, and a baby's smile.

MELCHIOR: Oh, please! That New-Age drivel is fine for Sunday school sermons, but I'm a Wise Man, and I'd like some hard proof, if you don't mind. I thought at least he might do a little miracle. Make a bush burn, turn a stick into a snake . . . *Something*.

GASPAR: He did that one trick when you pulled his finger.

BALTHAZAR: You've studied the Holy Scriptures, Melchior. Did it not all come to pass as was foretold by the prophets?

MELCHIOR: Prophets, shmophets. I've been thinking this through, and something smells awfully fishy. I mean, if God is his Father, then who is this Joseph character? He's supposed to be some Good Samaritan along for the ride? I don't think so. If you ask me, somebody sold us a real bill of goods here. How do we know this whole thing wasn't staged? I wouldn't be surprised if the government was behind it.

GASPAR: *(Aggressively.)* Hey! Watch it, Mel! We don't need that kind of subversive talk around here.

MELCHIOR: It's a free country.

BALTHAZAR: No it isn't. It's a Jewish puppet state under a Roman occupation.

GASPAR: That's right, and we don't need any commie agitators making waves. I've been on the road tracking down false Messiahs since 14 BC and as far as I'm concerned, this little squirt is the real McCoy. Case closed.

BALTHAZAR: BC? What's that?

GASPAR: That's the new reckoning of time. Everything's AD from here on in.

BALTHAZAR: So what is this, then? The year One, or the year Zero?

GASPAR: One, I suppose. Or no, maybe Zero. Because if the milennium starts in the year 1000 . . .

BALTHAZAR: No, doesn't the millenium start in 1001 . . . ?

MELCHIOR: See? We can't even figure out what year it is! And we're supposed to be Wise Men?

GASPAR: I thought we were Kings.

BALTHAZAR: That's right. We Three Kings of Orient are.

MELCHIOR: Have you looked in the mirror lately? You think you look Oriental?

*(To Gaspar.)*

Do you? Does any one of us look the slightest fucking bit Asian?

GASPAR: Hey, language. There's a baby inside.

MELCHIOR: Maybe. And maybe it's just a midget in a diaper. I've seen that dodge before. If he really is the King of Kings, what's he doing in this crummy stable?

GASPAR: It's technically a manger.

MELCHIOR: Manger, stable . . . whatever. Why isn't he staying over at the Bethlehem Arms?

BALTHAZAR: Because there's no room at the inn.

MELCHIOR: Oh, bullshit. There's always an extra room somewhere. All you have to do is pay off the concierge.

BALTHAZAR: But what about the star, Melchior? You followed the holy star, didn't you?

MELCHIOR: *(Dismissive.)* That's just an exploding supernova — an astronomical curiosity, nothing more. No, there's some kind of scam going on here. We're being set up for a fall, I'm telling you.

GASPAR: So what are we supposed to do about it?

MELCHIOR: *I'm* going home. Where I'm gonna just sit tight and keep my mouth shut. And I advise you two mugs to do the same.

BALTHAZAR: But we have to spread the word about the Messiah.

MELCHIOR: Why? What good is it going to do? You think the Romans are going to be happy about a Messiah muscling in on their territory? You think Herod's gonna do a back-flip when he finds out he ain't the King of the Jews anymore? This is political dynamite, fellas. And I wash my hands of it — whatever that means.

BALTHAZAR: I disagree, Melchior. I believe we are ushering in a New World Order, an age of peace on earth, and good will toward men.

GASPAR: Yes! The days of pagan barbarity are over. No more wars, no more atrocities, no more race hatred.

BALTHAZAR: And every man will be free to live the life he chooses, according to his own beliefs and sexual preferences.

GASPAR: *(Dubious.)* Well . . . I don't know about *that.*

BALTHAZAR: *(Amending his thought.)* We'll all try to be more tolerant, anyway.

MELCHIOR: You guys are nuts. This is the beginning of *more* intolerance, *more* persecution, *more* hatred. You will see armies rise up around the world to do battle against this new religion — and the streets will run red with the blood shed in his name. Torture, enslavement, genocide — all will follow in the wake of his gentle teachings. Yes, we've got trouble, my friends. Trouble with a capital *T,* and that rhymes with *P,* and that stands for . . . OK, I'm getting a little confused. But mark my words, this business can come to no good, and if we had any sense we'd burn down this manger and everyone in it. It's the end of the world, I tell you! The end of the world . . . !

*(Melchior rushes off in terror.)*

BALTHAZAR: He turned out to be a real wet blanket, didn't he?

GASPAR: Ahh, screw him. We can be the *Two* Kings instead. More money for us. Come on, let's get that drink.

*(He limps as he walks off.)*

Oy! I've got camel sores like you wouldn't believe.

BALTHAZAR: I have some aloe vera in my goatskin.

GASPAR: Oh, yeah? You wanna rub it on for me?

BALTHAZAR: What are you, a wise guy?

GASPAR: No, a "Wise Man" . . .

*(They both laugh, as they head off.)*

END OF PLAY

# Bruce

## C. DENBY SWANSON

*Bruce* by C. Denby Swanson was originally commissioned and produced for REVENGE by The Drilling Company, artistic director Hamilton Clancy. It was presented at 78th Street Theatre Lab in New York City, June 3, 2005, directed by Kate Moloy, with the following cast: Gail — Kim Donovan; Lawyer — Colleen Cosgrove; Dean — Dave Marantz.

CHARACTERS
>    GAIL
>    A LAWYER (female)
>    DEAN

SETTING
>    A house

· · ·

SCENE 1

*A house.*

LAWYER: I wish you had come to my office.

GAIL: We have to make up a story.

LAWYER: Gail, I can't make up a story —

GAIL: He will be home from work.

LAWYER: Gail —

GAIL: We have to have a story.

LAWYER: Next time, will you come to my office?

GAIL: No, I can't — I can't be gone when he gets home —

LAWYER: Jesus.

GAIL: We'll just tell him you're a long lost friend from college.

LAWYER: A long lost friend from college who has come by to show off some fancy legal filings?

GAIL: What do I need to sign? I'll sign it and — I'll sign whatever I have to, just —

LAWYER: Gail —

GAIL: He can't know.

LAWYER: Are you that scared of him?

GAIL: He just can't know.

LAWYER: We'll file for the divorce and get an order of protection.

GAIL: No, it's just —

LAWYER: I can take you someplace. He won't be able to find you.

GAIL: No —

LAWYER: I have lots of experience in this field, Gail, I know people. Trust me to help you.

GAIL: He doesn't —

LAWYER: What.

GAIL: He —

LAWYER: What.

(Pause.)

GAIL: If I leave, he'll do something to the pig.

LAWYER: The pig.

GAIL: Yes.

LAWYER: He'll do something to the pig?

GAIL: We had three, but —

LAWYER: But?

GAIL: Well.

LAWYER: I don't think I fully understand.

GAIL: He'll do something to it.

LAWYER: I think you should be worried about your own safety, Gail, that's what I think. The pig —

GAIL: I am. I am.

LAWYER: Alright. So we file based on a record of physical abuse.

GAIL: Abuse.

LAWYER: Yes.

GAIL: Not abuse but um —

LAWYER: Gail.

GAIL: It's not that.

(Silence.)

GAIL: He's going to be back soon.

(Lawyer stuffs her briefcase full of papers.)

GAIL: I don't have any proof but —

LAWYER: But what.

GAIL: I think he's given me something.

LAWYER: Given you something?

GAIL: Yes.

LAWYER: Like a disease?

GAIL: Um.

LAWYER: He's been unfaithful?

GAIL: He has —

LAWYER: Gail, come with me to a shelter. You don't need to bring anything. Just let me get you out of this house. I'll take you to a doctor, you'll get treated —

GAIL: If I'm not home when he gets back, he has gone out there and done — something with the pigs — he used to when there were three of them —

LAWYER: What?

GAIL: Done something —

LAWYER: Something —

GAIL: And then he brings it back in to me.

> *(A moment of silence.)*

LAWYER: Oh.

GAIL: I think — I think he is turning me into one of them. I think that is the result.

LAWYER: What?

GAIL: I think. I am turning. Into a pig.

LAWYER: Oh.

> *(They regard each other for a moment.)*
> *(A car door slams.)*
> *(GAIL jumps. She makes a pig snorting sound. It just comes out.)*

GAIL: Oh, no.

> *(She snorts again. She is overwhelmed by snorting.)*

GAIL: Oh, no. Oh, no.

LAWYER: It's alright, it's alright —

GAIL: Oh, no. Oh, no. Oh, no.

> *(Gail panics. She continues to snort. She gets very upset. The Lawyer tries to comfort her. Snorting. Crying. It's a mess.)*
> *(Dean enters.)*

DEAN: Honey?

> *(Gail freezes. Dean stares at the Lawyer.)*
> *(Silence.)*

LAWYER: I am a long lost friend from college.

## SCENE 2

> *Dinner. Dean and Gail sit opposite each other.*
> *Knives scrape.*
> *They eat.*

GAIL: How was your day?

> *(Dean shrugs. He eats.)*

GAIL: Good.

DEAN: It was good.

GAIL: Good.

DEAN: Pass the uh —

*(He gestures toward a serving bowl. Gail hands it to him.)*

GAIL: Mine, too.

DEAN: What.

GAIL: Good.

DEAN: Good.

GAIL: Quiet.

DEAN: Good.

GAIL: I had my cup of tea. Then I took my bath.

DEAN: Your bath.

GAIL: Yes.

DEAN: Your bath.

GAIL: Dean.

DEAN: Were you dirty?

GAIL: Dean, please —

DEAN: What.

GAIL: Please eat.

*(Dean stares at her.)*

GAIL: The food.

DEAN: Oh.

GAIL: It's getting cold.

*(Dean eats.)*

*(Gail considers her meal. She pushes the food into a thick line down its center.)*

DEAN: Not hungry?

GAIL: No.

*(Dean shrugs.)*

DEAN: More for the pigs.

*(He eats. She stares.)*

*(Then, Gail throws her head into the center of her plate and feeds from it as if it were a trough.)*

DEAN: That's better.

GAIL: Mmmm.

DEAN: S' Good, isn't it.

GAIL: Mmmhhhhmmm

DEAN: New recipe?

GAIL: Uhhhummh

DEAN: What is it?

*(Silence.)*

*(Gail takes her last bite. AH.)*

GAIL: Ham.

## SCENE 3

*A courtroom.*

LAWYER: Your Honor, as part of the divorce settlement, my client, the petitioner, is requesting custody of the couple's surviving pig.

It is a, well your standard pig, pink, with a — a snout — uh, and it's seven years old, about 350 pounds. There used to be other pigs but they — well, my client requests custody of the pig. I am submitting into the record a recent photograph of the pig that my client took.

Please excuse the obviously unimpressive photo processing, we had them do that one-hour thing in about twenty minutes, the kid at the counter was very young — they are all so young these days — and I think he just —

*(Pause.)*

LAWYER: My client is very specific about the term *custody*, she feels a significant bond with the animal and would to like to formally change its name to to — Bruce. Bruce. Which was her father's — uh — she feels a kind of parental responsibility — a kind of —

*(Pause.)*

LAWYER: Your Honor, honestly, this has been a very difficult case. There are many additional — conflicting — factors. I am distinctly aware of a certain hostility at work here between the three — uh — members of this family, shall we say — In fact my client is unable to make this proceeding because of mobility issues that developed after —

Early on, I tried to get her to leave the bastard but she refused. She refused. And now — now —

*(The Lawyer looks down at her notes and cannot continue.)*

LAWYER: Your Honor, may I approach?

END OF PLAY

# PLAYS FOR
# FOUR ACTORS

# Three Guys and a Brenda

ADAM BOCK

CHARACTERS

> BOB: a man, played by a woman
> JOE: a man, played by a woman
> RANDALL: a man, played by a woman
> BRENDA: a woman, played by a woman

SETTING

> At work

. . .

*Before this, Bob, Joe and Randall were watching TV waiting for their shift to start.*
*Now:*

> *Bob and Joe are onstage. They are crying.*
> *Randall walks across stage, crying. Exits.*
> *Bob and Joe continue to cry.*
> *Randall walks onstage. He is still crying. He has a roll of toilet tissue.*
> *He hands out tissue. They are all crying.*
> *Brenda walks across stage. They try not to/don't cry when she is onstage.*
> *She exits.*
> *They cry again. Deep breaths.*
> *They sniff. They sniff. They sniff.*
> *Brenda enters.*

BRENDA: You guys are on second shift right?

JOE: Yeah Brenda.

BOB: Yeah that's right.

BRENDA: Joe, then when your shift starts, then you and Bob are going to show Randall what to do with the new machine, OK?

JOE: OK.

BRENDA: OK?

BOB: Yeah OK.

JOE: OK sure.

BRENDA: OK then.

> *(Exits.)*

JOE: *(Deep breath, doesn't cry.)* Fucking animal nature shows.

BOB: I know.

JOE: They get me every time.

RANDALL: She's so beautiful.

JOE: She is.

BOB: She is Randall.

JOE: Yes she is.

RANDALL: Isn't she Bob? She's beautiful!

BOB: She is Randall.

RANDALL: I have to tell her she's beautiful.

BOB: I don't know Randall.

JOE: I don't know.

BOB: What do you think Joe?

JOE: I don't know about that Bob.

BOB: Yeah me neither I don't know either.

JOE: Might not be appropriate. In the work environment.

BOB: Right.

JOE: Right?

BOB: In the work environment.

JOE: This being work.

BOB: Right.

RANDALL: I have to.

BOB: Well if you have to, you have to.

JOE: That's right.

BOB: If you have to, you have to.

JOE: Right.

BOB: Right.

JOE: But I don't think you're going to.

BOB: Nope.

JOE: Right?

BOB: Nope!

RANDALL: I have to.

BOB: Joe here might.

JOE: That's something I might tell her.

BOB: Right. Joe might.

JOE: I might. I might say something to her like

BOB: Like

JOE: "You're beautiful!"

BOB: Right!

JOE: But I don't know whether you'd say something like that.

RANDALL: I am too. I am too going to say something like that to her!

JOE: Well.

BOB: Well.

JOE: Well OK then.

RANDALL: Because I think she's beautiful.

BOB: Well.

JOE: OK then.

RANDALL: And I'm going to say it.

BOB: OK then.

JOE: OK.

> *(Randall exits.)*

JOE: Think he's going to tell her?

BOB: Nope.

JOE: I'm not watching any more of those nature shows. They're too sad.

BOB: Yeah I know. Me neither.

JOE: They're too fucking sad. They make me sad.

RANDALL: *(To audience.)* Thing that's hard about being a guy? You always have to tell the girl "Hey you're great" or "Hey I think you're great" or "You're great" or "You're great" and "Would you maybe want to go out?" and that's hard.

> Plus it's hard to have to shave all the time. That's hard too.

JOE: *(To audience.)* Plus it's hard to pick a good deodorant.

RANDALL: *(To audience.)* Yeah that's hard too.

JOE: *(To audience.)* Plus guys? Plus we have to carry everything.

RANDALL: *(To audience.)* Right.

JOE: *(To audience.)* Especially heavy things. Like sofas.

RANDALL: *(To audience.)* Yeah that's hard.

BOB: *(To audience.)* Plus

JOE: *(To audience.)* Plus you have to drive all the time.

RANDALL: *(To audience.)* Yeah. And that.

BOB: *(To audience.)* Plus

JOE: *(To audience.)* You have to drive on really long trips, to the beach, to visit your family, and then back from the beach. And if a tire blows you have to take it off, you have to put the spare on. Plus you have to pay.

RANDALL: *(To audience.)* For everything.

BOB: *(To audience.)* Plus

JOE: *(To audience.)* Plus sometimes you don't understand something and that can make you feel stupid and so you have to pretend you understand it. That can be hard.

> *(Pause.)*

BOB: Yeah.

RANDALL: Yeah.

> *(Pause.)*

JOE: *(To audience.)* That can be hard.

> *(Pause.)*

RANDALL: *(To audience.)* Mostly it's hard though saying "I think you're great" and "Would you maybe like to go out" and then you have to wait and find out what the answer is. That's hard.

> *(Brenda enters.)*

RANDALL: Um. Brenda?

BRENDA: Give me a second.

> *(Brenda exits.)*

RANDALL: Guys. Don't bust my chops.

JOE: I didn't say anything.

RANDALL: Don't bust my chops.

> *(Brenda enters.)*

RANDALL: Hey Brenda?

BRENDA: I said just give me a.

> *(She exits. Joe, Bob, and Randall stand.)*
> *(Randall looks at Joe and Bob.)*
> *(Brenda enters.)*

BRENDA: Yeah OK?

RANDALL: Oh yeah so. Um.

BRENDA: Yeah?

RANDALL: Guys?

JOE: Oh yeah.

BOB: What?

JOE: OK. Come on.

BOB: What?

JOE: Bob come on.

BOB: Oh yeah yeah OK!

JOE: OK!

BOB: OK.

> *(They exit.)*

RANDALL: Yeah so Brenda?

BRENDA: Yeah OK?

RANDALL: So.

BRENDA: I have work Randall.

RANDALL: Um.

BRENDA: Yeah OK so, what?

RANDALL: Um.

BRENDA: I have work.

> (*Turns to exit.*)

RANDALL: I think you're beautiful.

BRENDA: What?

RANDALL: Um.

BRENDA: That's not funny.

RANDALL: What?

BRENDA: That's not funny.

RANDALL: I'm not being funny.

BRENDA: That's mean. That pisses me off. That really truly pisses me off.

RANDALL: No I do.

BRENDA: I have a lot of work. And you're pissing me off.

RANDALL: No I do. I think you're beautiful. I think you're beautiful like a. Like something beautiful. Like the sun in the sky. Like a lake. Like the sunshine on a lake in the early evening right before the sun goes down and everything is calm. And the water's calm. That's what I think.

BRENDA: Shut up.

RANDALL: No I do.

BRENDA: Like a lake?

RANDALL: Like the sunshine. On the lake.

BRENDA: Really?

RANDALL: Yeah really.

BRENDA: Really?

RANDALL: And I think "If only I could kiss her I'd be happy."

BRENDA: Really?

RANDALL: Yeah.

BRENDA: You think if you kissed me, you'd be happy?

RANDALL: Yeah.

BRENDA: You want to kiss me?

RANDALL: Yeah.

BRENDA: And that would make you happy?

RANDALL: Yeah.

BRENDA: Just a kiss?

RANDALL: Yeah.

BRENDA: OK so.

RANDALL: Really?

BRENDA: So?

*(They kiss. Should be a good smooch.)*

RANDALL: *(Softly.)* Yeah. That made me happy.

BRENDA: I have work.

RANDALL: OK.

BRENDA: I have work.

RANDALL: OK. OK.

*(She exits.)*

JOE: *(To audience.)* I told my wife I loved the sound of her voice on the phone. And I do. I still do.

BOB: *(To audience.)* I gave my girlfriend a smooth stone I found on the side of the road.

JOE: Right?

BOB: Yeah.

RANDALL: *Smiles.*

*(The three men sit.)*


END OF PLAY

# Second Kiss

## Andrea Lepcio

*Second Kiss* by Andrea Lepcio was performed as part of Vital
Signs New Works Festival, ArtsPass in Process Week,
December 15–18, 2005 at Vital Theatre Compan: Stephen
Sunderlin, Artistic Director; Linda Ames Key, Producing
Director. Curator/Producer was Linda Ames Key. Producing
Director/Co-producer was Nicole Godino. Stage Manager was
Pamela Salling. Lighting Designer was Rie Ono. Scenic
Designer was Jessica Hooks. The director was Stephanie
Gilman. The cast was as follows:  Best Friend — Ellen
Crowley-Etten; Me — Jenny Gammelllo; Girl — Jenna
Kalinowski; Boy — Will Reynolds. AEA The Vital production
was part of the 31st Annual Samuel French Festival where Boy
was played by Nathan Williams.

CHARACTERS

> ME: a just-turned sixteen-year-old girl
> BEST FRIEND: eighth grader
> BOY: a seventeen-year-old boy
> GIRL: an eighteen-year-old girl

TIME

> Anytime and not-so-distant past

SETTING

> School yard, coffee shop, down the path

NOTE

> Since most one-act festivals involve many actors, many of whom are young, the play calls for as many couples as the company can spare to make out, hook up, and otherwise flirt around the main character.

• • •

ME: I am sweet sweet sixteen and I have never been, never been, never. A lot of things actually never mind kissed which I haven't cause I don't count "seven minutes in heaven" rubbing dry lips mush mush with Steven Kurtz in the fifth grade or my cousin Barry's bar mitzvah when the DJ made us play dance/freeze and his obnoxious girlfriend Karen got the bright idea to stick me and Mitchell Drecker's braces together. I've never been kissed. And, really, see, I don't . . . I don't even get it. Kissing. This . . . I don't know. This wanting to kiss . . . maybe I'm retarded.
*(As many actors as the company can spare make out, hook up, and otherwise flirt.)*
*(Back then, eighth grade.)*
BEST FRIEND: Lora Tosk went all the way.
ME: All the way where?
BEST FRIEND: She did it.
ME: Did what?
BEST FRIEND: With a sophomore.
ME: I don't understand, I don't understand.
BEST FRIEND: Lora Tosk had sex.
ME: You mean
BEST FRIEND: Yeah

ME: Like with a

BEST FRIEND: Penis.

ME: I had to think about that a lot. A lot and still, to this day, when I see Lora Tosk. I mean, every single time, even now, years later when I don't see her every day but only just Tuesdays and Thursdays in Spanish. Every time I see her all I think is Lora Tosk *había sexo en octova grado.*

    I understood the principle. The procedure in theory, but I still didn't, don't have any feel for it or interest which is very confusing to not at all give a shit about something that most every other person I know and like the rest of the planet . . .

*(The frolicking gets serious.)*

ME: *(Continued.)* . . . it's not like I haven't tried. It's not like I haven't explored my hand brushing by my nipples under my sheet. I've reached all the way down to like find the parts. My parts. And the nipples or whatever I briefly brush. Probably too briefly. Feeling something disconnected from anything I know. But liking a little bit the idea of someone telling me to do something as in making me.

*(Boy breaks out of another girl's arms, turns to Me.)*

BOY: Come here. Watcha doing.

ME: Sitting. Nothing. Going.

BOY: So like that was weird with your party, your parents being there.

ME: They surprised me.

BOY: And then they stayed.

ME: It was my birthday.

BOY: Weird.

ME: I guess.

BOY: How'd they even get you to the party?

ME: Uh . . . they just took me to the restaurant.

BOY: But how'd they like know where you were?

ME: I was home.

BOY: Don't you go out?

ME: Sure, yeah, sometimes.

BOY: You want to go.

ME: Right now?

BOY: Yes.

ME: Where?

BOY: I don't know.

ME: Oh.

BOY: Get a soda.

ME: I guess.

BOY: A raspberry lime rickey. Why are you laughing?

ME: It's just a joke. My best friend. From my old school.
We used to call it. Back in eighth grade. We used to go to Friendly's and we'd call it . . . I don't know, one of us made a mistake one time so we called it a raspberry lime lickey.

BOY: A lickey.

ME: Stupid.

BOY: I like lickeys.

ME: Yeah.

BOY: Do you like lickeys?

ME: I like ginger ale better.

BOY: Let's sit at the counter.

ME: I've never been here.

BOY: No?

ME: We don't come here. We haven't.

BOY: Who?

ME: My family. My parents, I guess.

BOY: Do you go everywhere with them?

ME: No. Sometimes. Well like —

BOY: One Raspberry Lime Lickey, please.

ME: One Raspberry Lime Rickey.

BOY: Don't you want to share?

ME: Oh, OK.
*(Drink arrives.)*

BOY: Like this.
*(Sticks straws in.)*

BOY: *(Continued.)* One for me and one for you.

ME: Oh, kay. Funny.
*(They drink.)*

BOY: Lick

ME: Lickey.

BOY: Lick.

ME: Lickey.

BOY: Lick.

ME: He just licked me. Flicked me with his tongue.

BOY: Raspberry.

ME: Top lip.

BOY: Lime.

ME: Bottom lip.

BOY: Lickey.

ME: Tongue.

BOY: Tongue.

ME: Thick, poking.

BOY: Rise, blood, filling, filling.

ME: Poke.

BOY: Wanting, wanting.

ME: Poke. Poke.

BOY: Wanting!!!!!!!

ME: I don't get it.

BOY: See you.

ME: Yeah, OK.

　　　*(Boy hooks up with someone else.)*

ME: *(Continued.)* I have always liked being by myself, have always had things
　　　to do so I guess that's a good thing since I don't really like anyone half
　　　as much as everyone else seems to
　　　*(Very loaded.)*
　　　like each other.
　　　*(A new Girl approaches. She has not been part of the crowd.)*

GIRL: You see the maple.

ME: Yeah.

GIRL: The one behind the field, down the path.

ME: Past the bog.

GIRL: Near the rock.

ME: That's my rock.

GIRL: That's my tree.

ME: You have a tree?

GIRL: You have a rock?

ME: Sometimes a tree.

GIRL: Sometimes a rock.

ME: Since I could walk.

GIRL: Since I could crawl.

ME: Since I was born.

GIRL: Since forever.

ME: I used to leave my ma's womb at night to go sit on my rock.

GIRL: I waited in that tree till my folks fucked to make me.

ME: I'm . . . out . . . .

GIRL: I'll show you my tree if you show me your rock.

ME: OK.

GIRL: Now?

ME: Now. Yeah.

GIRL: Come on.

ME: Butterflies.

GIRL: Wonder.

ME: Something. Something. Something.

GIRL: Hurry.

ME: Last one.

GIRL: Last one.

ME: Racing.

GIRL: Breath.

ME: Heart.

GIRL: Beat.

ME: Beating.

GIRL: I like this rock.

ME: I like this tree.

GIRL: There's only one thing wrong.

ME: You have to go home?

GIRL: I'm eighteen.

ME: I know.

GIRL: Eighteen year olds don't have to . . . anything.

ME: I have to a lot of things.

GIRL: I know.

ME: Then what's wrong?

GIRL: You're over there.

ME: You're over there.

GIRL: Tree or rock?

ME: Tree.

GIRL: Here I come.

ME: OK.

GIRL: Quick.

ME: Lips.

GIRL: Tongue.

ME: Luscious.

I didn't know I knew that word, I didn't know, I didn't know.

GIRL: Luscious.

ME: More.

GIRL: Sweet.

ME: More.
GIRL: Salt.
ME: More.
GIRL: Yummy.
ME: You.
GIRL: You.
ME: Stay.
GIRL: Stay.
ME: Stay.
>I get it.
>*(Out.)*
>I get it.
>*(Back to Girl.)*
>I get it.
>*(Curtain.)*

END OF PLAY

# Cardinal Rule

## EMILY DEVOTI

*Cardinal Rule* was created and performed for The Orchard Project and The 24 Hour Company, August 2006. Directed by Ted Sperling. The original cast: Lydia — Naomi Frederick; Jeremy — Mike Szeles; Susanna — Melissa Leo; Gemma — Romi Diaz.

## CHARACTERS

LYDIA
JEREMY
SUSANNA
GEMMA

•   •   •

*Lydia, slightly pregnant, stands on stage, very still, with her hand out.*

LYDIA: They say if you stand still long enough, they'll settle. On your palm. If you put seed there. Good seed. Especially if it's a kind they really like. You can research that. For the particular bird? If you sweeten your palm enough, you can even get a lady cardinal, that's what they say. Usually ground feeders. But if you sweeten up your palm . . . and take away everything else around them, all the possibilities? If you take away their friends, scorch the earth, and vacuum up all the little natural grubs and worms and things? Well, then, if you stand still long enough, reeeeeal still, they'll settle.

JEREMY: Lydia, there you are. I was calling and calling —

LYDIA: I was being quiet.

JEREMY: I can see that.

LYDIA: I was being still.

JEREMY: I thought maybe we could go to town and —

LYDIA: You scared the birds away.

*(Shift:)*

LYDIA: "The North American cardinal, though a seed-eating bird, consumes a notable number of insects, particularly in breeding season. In the wild, attractive plants include greenbriar, Eastern red cedar, American holly, wild grape, hackberry . . . "

*(Susanna takes over the monologue. She's sitting next to Lydia now, reading out of her book.)*

SUSANNA: " . . . tussock sedge, smooth sumac, Virginia creeper . . . But above all, cardinals show a strong preference for unhulled sunflower seeds, and may often be observed at feeding stations, scratching away all other seeds to find them. They also eat safflower seeds, white proso millet, field cricket, true katydid, differential grasshopper . . . peanut butter . . . "

Where did you pick up this shit?

*(She lights a cigarette.)*

LYDIA: It's about the local landscape. It's natural. I'm trying to blend. It's what people read around here, isn't it?

SUSANNA: I don't know, I always read Bukowski. You ever read Bukowski?

*(Lydia takes a pocket of seeds from her pocket and starts to eat them, hulling them with her teeth.)*

SUSANNA: What about the birds?

LYDIA: *(Thinking she means the seeds.)* Trying to stop. Smoking.

*(She shells and spits the seeds, voraciously.)*

SUSANNA: No, I mean, why cardinals? I'd peg you for something lighter.

LYDIA: I like the way they hide behind their mates. Let them go out there and take the heat.

SUSANNA: Chickadee, or lighter even, a swallow or —

LYDIA: They blend into the woods and scrub, safe.

SUSANNA: Hummingbird, that's it. Ruby-throated.

LYDIA: But when you look real close, they're the colors of a chiffon scarf, like from the forties, you know? Old landscapes with bleeding colors and . . . and fawns. Green into red and yet the last thing you think about when you look at them is Christmas. How do they do that? It takes real grace to pull that off. Like . . . like Greta Garbo or something — but mostly, it's 'cause they like the seeds. I need them, I — you know, the whole oral — Jeremy doesn't know I smoke.

SUSANNA: It's OK. Gemma doesn't know I come here to visit you, so we all have our little secrets, now, don't we?

*(She blows smoke in her face, seductively.)*

Oh, sorry — didn't mean to tempt you.

*(She takes another drag, this time blows the smoke out of the other corner of her mouth.)*

You weave intricate webs, don't you, dearie?

LYDIA: What do you mean?

SUSANNA: Smoke screens.

*(As the scene shifts:)*

SUSANNA: I used to sit alone, in the dark, with my knife, army issue, sharp, lean. And I'd spin it, Bukowski taught me that, clear my mind, watch it, till it picked up speed, became solid almost, a circle, flashing and gleaming, refracting the light from the camp . . .

*(Susanna disappears.)*

JEREMY: Any luck?

*(Lydia jolts. She wipes her mouth, trying to hide the seed crumbs. She shifts the sunflower seeds in her hands.)*

JEREMY: You should wait till winter, you know. You'll have a better shot.

LYDIA: Less options, is what you mean.

JEREMY: Works every time.

LYDIA: Desperation.

JEREMY: You know, we didn't need to come out here. It's supposed to be a getaway. A good thing.

LYDIA: I'm good.

*(Flashes a too-good smile.)*

JEREMY: Lydia?

*(She thinks he's going to ask her something serious. She's tense.)*

LYDIA: Yeah?

JEREMY: You've got something — right . . . left tooth. No, it's — here, let me —

LYDIA: I'm OK, I'm —

*(He sticks his finger in her tooth, and expertly swipes the detritus out. Looks at his finger.)*

JEREMY: *(Perplexed.)* It's a husk.

*(Shift:)*

SUSANNA: Not many women in the army. I did it for the boots. Back in college. ROTC. And the scholarship. And . . . well, it was the boots really. If you grew up here, you'd understand, I mean — we didn't have much back then. I mean, we shared everything. And I know, that's a good thing, now that's considered good parenting and all, but when you're — I mean, when you're the fourth kid in a family of five kids, and you've never ripped a tag off your clothes yourself . . . your own new boots mean something different to you, is all I'm saying.

*(Takes a drag.)*

So does getting *out.*

*(Shift:)*

SUSANNA: *(To Lydia.)* I can take you to the field.

LYDIA: There's plenty of fields. I can find them myself.

SUSANNA: No, the Field. The Great Field. Woodstock. We used to go there, when I was a teenager, we used to . . . lie on the ground, and try to remember. We weren't actually there at the time, but, they all came to US, this little remote, I mean — *nothing* came to us — and our parents, they weren't around for it. They were, but see, Woodstock? That happened when I was just a kid, you know, and not more than ten miles away, but . . . How can I say this? Time and place is a relative thing. Something can be happening for you, five feet away from me, five inches, five centimeters . . . and it's not happening for me. And a Happening, well. You had to be of a certain — let's just say it wasn't, not for my folks, not then, not . . . Happening? I don't think so. But when I was a teenager —

*(Laughs.)*

We'd lie on that field, and we'd just . . . try to soak it all in.

LYDIA: What was it like?

SUSANNA: It was red, muted. And green, sometimes, when the sun hit right, when — new recruits came. Sand as far as you can — the colors bled.

*(Phone rings from another part of the stage. Beat.)*

LYDIA: I meant Woodstock.

SUSANNA: I don't know. I wasn't there.

*(Shift:)*

*(Gemma, at home, picks up the phone.)*

GEMMA: Hello? Oh, Derek. Well, what a surprise. Yeah, well, I — so, how are you and Claudia?

*(Susanna stands at the corner of the room, watching. Gemma doesn't see her.)*

Oh, in vitro, sure. Still sticking it to her, eh? The hormones, I meant the — hormones. Right. It wasn't, actually, a joke, it was just — well, glad that's working out for you.

*(Gemma suddenly sees Susanna, her face lights up.)*

*(Whispers to Susanna.)*

Hi. Weird. I'll tell you, I'll —

*(Back to phone.)*

Oh, I'm fine. We're — yeah. We . . . *happy*, we're — I'm — you know, it's really good to hear your voice. I mean, when Trevor and I —

*(Whispers to Susanna.)*

Sorry.

*(To phone.)*

Yeah, well, all our old friends, all MY old — I mean. I thought you guys were my — Anyhow, I'm really glad now — Oh . . . Yeah, well, I don't know much about Fantasy Football, no, you're right. I'm probably not the best — Oh . . .

*(She's crestfallen.)*

Oh . . . You thought — yeah, you might want to fix that. On your phone. It's simple, you just — Yeah, this is MY cell. Our number was, is — right. 867 . . . You got it.

*(Her face drops, as she listens.)*

Yeah, well, it's still good to talk to you. I'm glad you — say hi to Claudia, I'll —

*(The phone goes dead, she puts it down.)*

Bye.

*(She tries to be upbeat but she can't.)*

He didn't mean to call me. I thought —

SUSANNA: I thought you left the breeders behind you.

GEMMA: Where were you?

SUSANNA: In the field.

*(As the scene shifts:)*

SUSANNA: And I'd sit there, and wait, alone in the dark, for the knife to stop spinning, for the answers to come . . .

JEREMY: There's something happening. Lately. All my friends, their wives are — I don't know. Different than when we first. I mean, back in college. They were so — I don't know, sweet, so . . . I mean, smart, but . . . I mean, docile, kind of. You know? They were so . . .

But lately, they, I don't know if it's age or what, but, it's coming out. Of their pores. Of their — like some old primordial force. It's like they hit their thirties and whooooa. Whoa. I don't know what to say.

*(Lydia steps on.)*

JEREMY: Write a story, a short one.

LYDIA: I'm good. I'm baking. I'm —

JEREMY: Work on your creativity — bring it back.

LYDIA: Canning, pickling —

JEREMY: You were always so beautiful when you wrote. You were so happy.

LYDIA: — jarring things.

JEREMY: I loved to watch you write.

LYDIA: I don't need to do that any more. I live in the country. I'm a housewife. I left that be — [hind]

JEREMY: Before you came here, before we — you used to write all the time, I just think if you —

LYDIA: I said I left that behind. OK? I am *happy*, Jeremy. Don't push it.

JEREMY: I thought we'd start new. I thought. Somewhere wholesome. Our own. Rich soil. Deep earth. Perfect place to —

LYDIA: Plant roots.

JEREMY: Right.

LYDIA: We'll get a cow!

JEREMY: Chickens.

LYDIA: Grow our own vegetables.

JEREMY: Raise a family.

*(He puts his hand on her belly. She flinches.)*

LYDIA: Like nothing ever happened.

*(Shift:)*

SUSANNA: When I went into the army, I thought I'd never come back. This landscape, the mountains, cool and deep like water. It used to hem me in, you know? Like it was a wall higher than any ropes course we had to scale. Not that you have to scale things in the army these days. It's more about kicking in doors, and riding in vehicles. Strapping on ammunition. Things I wouldn't be opposed to, mind you — they had their charm. But something happened this time. When the earth got hot. Suddenly, this place started to well up inside of me. And now?

LYDIA: He doesn't know it, but Susanna grew up here. So when he suggested we move here — ! She used to tell me about it. Slip next to me, and describe it. Slip next to me . . . She hated it here. I think part of me wanted to come here, perversely, because I wanted to feel her hate. Hate sometimes, after all, is stronger, than love. It's more specific. More tangible. It tells you who someone adamantly is not.

SUSANNA: I would do anything to be here, really be here, in the moment, in the present. Looking at the peaks and mountains. No sand, slipping through. No mirages. Memories. Bleeding colors . . .

GEMMA: When I met her, she'd had her heart broken. Someone had left her, for another narrative — something a little more traditional, a little more ingrained. It made her, a little more fragile. Than she ever was again. With me. I didn't leave Trevor for her. I mean, could you imagine, if I had? I mean, I'm a widow. She made me. A war widow! Not that anyone around here would — Acknowledge that. She comes to me sometimes. I feel her. In the room. But then, she slips away. And I don't know where she went.

LYDIA: The praying mantid, when she's done mating? I hear she eats her prey, head first, then one spindly limb at a time. I don't know why she does that. Life's cycles, you know. Need. It's a relative term. What we feel in the moment. Something organic, you know? But when it's out of our system, this biology, then who are we? See, animals have it easy. They breed, and then they die. Breed and die, breed and die. But humans, see, we found a way to extend all that. Beyond nature. The biological imperative. And so we have Time. All this extra, after-the-fact Time . . . to pursue that which is beyond our need. To follow interests. To make a mess of things. I left her. Too soon. And now? I've forgotten what for.

*(Lydia sits at the table, and writes. She smiles, and really looks happy.)*

SUSANNA: But the knife didn't stop. And letting it spin, I turned away, and
realized he was right:
"You're going to have
to save yourself," Kid.

*(Lydia folds her note on the table, and leaves.)*

LYDIA: I can't get her out of my mind.

SUSANNA: Lydia?

JEREMY: *(Calls onto the empty porch.)* Lydia?

GEMMA: *(Calls out into the empty living room.)* Susanna?

LYDIA: Where have you been?

*(Jeremy picks up a note, reads:)*

JEREMY: "For sale. Baby shoes. Never worn."

*(Lydia wraps a red scarf around her neck.)*

*(She and Susanna lay on the field, opposite sides of the stage, and take in the
past.)*

END OF PLAY

# Trojan Horse

MOLLY SMITH METZLER

Trojan Horse was first produced at Tisch School of the Arts
(N.Y.U.) by First Look Theatre Company in January 2006,
directed by Janice Goldberg, with the following cast:
Kate — Christina Denzinger; Kenny — Michael J. Reilly;
Brenda — Dina Comolli; Matthew — Zachary Booth.

CHARACTERS
    KATE: forty-three
    KENNY: fifty
    BRENDA: thirty-eight
    MATTHEW: fifteen

SETTING
    Kate's suburban New England living room

TIME
    The present. 9:30 PM on a Wednesday night

•   •   •

*AT RISE: Kate sits in a lotus position, deep breathing, listening to the sounds of a rain-forest serenity meditation tape. She is om. This is the peaceful scene until Kenny pounds the door wildly.*

KENNY: *(Offstage.)* KATE! It's Kenny! OPEN UP!

KATE: She's not home.

KENNY: I know you're home, Kate. Stop fucking around. Your car's in the driveway.

KATE: She's channeling negative energy.

*(Kate gives him the finger. Kenny pounds.)*

KENNY: *(Pound.)* Kate!

    *(Pound.)*

    Kate!

    *(Pound.)*

    Kate!

    *(Exasperated, she opens the door.)*

KATE: For God's sake, what!

    *(Kenny tears past her. He wears only boxer shorts, a ratty bathrobe, slippers, and a backpack. There's a little shaving cream on the side of his chin. He swings a baseball bat around as he shouts. Brenda follows meekly her husband.)*

KENNY: WHERE'S YOUR SON? I'm gonna bust his skull.

KATE: Excuse me!?

    *(Kenny pounds his bat on something.)*

KENNY: MATTHEW? SHOW YOUR FACE, BOY. We're going mano à
mano.

*(Kenny makes toward the stairs. Kate blocks the path.)*

KATE: Kenny! Stop right there!

KENNY: Move aside, Kate!

KATE: He isn't here! Who the hell do you think you —

KENNY: He isn't here?

KATE: No! He is not here!

KENNY: Funny. Cuz I called Will and he told me it's your night with him. So
you better bring the boy forth.

KATE: This is not how this is going to go! You don't get to barge in here after
a year to interrogate me. A year of no contact, no holiday cards, no dinner parties, not so much as a "Kate, do you need me to shovel your
walk?"

KENNY: I'm here about Matthew. This is not about you and Will's split.

KATE: We didn't split. He did. I didn't cheat. He did. And fuck you for not
honoring the difference, Kenny.

*(Beat.)*

BRENDA: Pumpkin? Ohh, I know: Let's e-mail Matthew. We're real sorry we
bothered you, Kate.

KENNY: I know he's upstairs. I see his light on. Maybe you didn't hear me,
Kate. I said Move. Aside.

KATE: Will might've let you bust in here like a retarded bull with that bat, but
there's a new sheriff in town, baby. You take one step, I swear I'll get you
arrested for trespassing and assault before you can blink.

*(Brenda clears her throat, indicates "Let's go, Kenny.")*

KATE: If you want to talk to me about my son, you can step outside, lose the
bat, and knock like a gentleman this time.

*(Kenny growls then exits. Brenda makes to follow him, but he slams the door,
trapping her in the living room. Awkward silence.)*

BRENDA: *(Nervous.)* I have no idea what he's on about, you know. He yanked
me from bed screaming something about killing Matthew and took off
running down the block.

*(Pause.)*

But it works out sorta nice because we get a little chat in. I haven't seen
you! I don't even know what you think of our kids dating. Aren't they
Barbie and Ken?

KATE: You've seen me.

BRENDA: Really? No! Where.

KATE: You see me all the time. ShopRite. Wal-Mart. At the Y.

BRENDA: Loop-de-loo. Brenda vision.

KATE: Oh, I'm pretty sure you see me.

*(Beat.)*

BRENDA: The house looks real nice, Kate. I like what you did with the trim there along the eh trim.

*(Carefully.)*

I've been meaning to come by.

KATE: But you've been busy. Dinners with Will and his new girlfriend that you two are so chummy with. What's her name?

BRENDA: Oh . . . Janine?

KATE: Yes, oh young Janine. I see your car over at their place. The double date BBQs that go on. I know who got the best friends in the divorce.

*(Kenny knocks. Kate answers the door.)*

KATE: Yes?

KENNY: *(Grumbles.)* . . . Canicomein?

KATE: Yes. Would you like to sit down?

KENNY: Yes.

*(Kenny sits.)*

KENNY: *(An order.)* Brenda.

*(Brenda runs and sits down next to him.)*

KATE: Now. What seems to be the problem?

*(Kenny unzips his bag.)*

KENNY: Oh God.

*(Losing ability to be contained.)*

I was shaving. I ran outta blades. So I went under the bathroom sink to find one of Brenda's, and there they were!

*(Pulling condom box out of backpack.)*

Look!

KATE: A box of Trojans.

KENNY: Count 'em!

KATE: One, two.

KENNY: TWO! Which means twenty-two are missing.

KATE: . . . You stud?

KENNY: No; um, no. Brenda and I haven't done it in wee . . . months.

BRENDA: Kenny.

KENNY: Been working a lot and our schedules, not to be graphic here or anything . . . This was an unopened box! They're doing it Kate! Matthew and Jennifer! He's been sneaking in and stealing them! From me — from her father!

KATE: I talk to Matthew about sex all the time. He says "Not me, not now."

KENNY: Don't you watch *Law & Order?* Any of 'em?

*(Pointing to condoms.)*

Evidence! They're going at it like bunnies. Porn bunnies.

KATE: Maybe — since your rubbers were in storage since the Ice Age — you lost count? Or maybe Jennifer gave them to a loose friend. Or maybe they're making balloons . . .

*(Brenda raises her hand, wanting to be heard.)*

KENNY: He steals my condoms, comes over here, puts them on his grubby penis, and screws my baby Jennifer. Here! Where he won't be caught by the slack single mom.

*(Calling on her.)*

Yes, Brenda.

BRENDA: Kenny —

KATE: I'll need to hear that last part again. Slack?

KENNY: When at our house, they're not allowed upstairs. When at his father and Janine's, they've got supervision —

BRENDA: Kenny, could I say —

KATE: You're using Will as the model parent? —

KENNY: And so, Brenda and me have decided that Jennifer can't come here anymore.

KATE: You're not going to let Jennifer come here anymore?

BRENDA: You're not?

KENNY: No.

KATE: To her second home since she was born.

KENNY: No.

KATE: Because you can't count your condoms?

KENNY: Because we can't count on you without Will.

*(Beat.)*

KATE: Brenda?

KENNY: She agrees.

BRENDA: I have to agree.

*(Beat.)*

KATE: What if I were to tell you that your daughter sleeps over here almost every night. She sneaks out of your house around ten o'clock.

KENNY: What?

KATE: She comes over and sleeps on the couch. If she's really upset, I even let her stay in Matthew's room —

KENNY: You what! —

KATE: Because I know — I trust! — that my son isn't touching her.

KENNY: Let me get this straight: You let my teenage daughter sleep in a bed with your teenage son because "she's upset"?

KATE: She's not stupid. She sees you two going into separate bedrooms. She hears doors slamming and things breaking. Of course she's upset.

KENNY: You're a liar! We are very . . . content.

BRENDA: No we're not.

KENNY: You got no business butting into our affairs, Kate!

BRENDA: She's taking care of our daughter, Ken —

KENNY: Will's right about you. You were OK for a couple years, but you're a washed up, meddling hag now.

KATE: Will's right about you too, Kenny. He says you're cut from the same mold and you sure damn are.

KENNY: C'mon Brenda. When Will hears about the teen sex parlor you're running, he'll get full custody of Matthew.

*(Not happy to repeat.)*

C'MON BRENDA.

BRENDA: Matthew didn't take your Trojans, Kenny. I did. I took them. It was me.

*(Beat.)*

BRENDA: I took them. They're missing because I used them. I . . . used them.

KENNY: To do what?

*(Kenny processes.)*

KENNY: You're cheating on me?

BRENDA: Yes.

KENNY: . . . twenty-two times?

*(Beat.)*

KENNY: Who is it?

BRENDA: It doesn't matter.

KENNY: The fuck it doesn't matter. It matters! Who is it?

BRENDA: It could be anybody. What do you need a name for? I could be fucking the pope. You still wouldn't have noticed. I packed everything but my flesh and left you months ago. You didn't notice. I cry from the moment I make morning coffee to the moment to I lie down to sleep. I spend money on manicures, and pedicures, and waxes, and thongs, and gym, and Pilates tapes and I walk around our house aching for you to look up and see me — to see me! — and you don't. Damn right I made love to him; I made love to him with your condoms right under your nose and all you noticed was that your property was stolen from under your sink!

*(Brenda makes toward the door. Then turns back.)*

BRENDA: *(To Kate.)* Thank you for being kind to Jennifer. Next time I see you I will say hello, and I hope you will someday say hello back.

*(Beat.)*

And Will's a fucker.

*(To Kenny.)*

I'll be at my sister's.

*(Brenda exits. Long beat.)*

KATE: Huh.

KENNY: My wife is cheating on me and I'm in your living room. In my underpants. This is the lowest. Gutter. Pavement. Dog shit on the pavement. She's just . . . poof?

KATE: Yeah.

KENNY: What now? I go home to an empty house? What do I do with an empty house? A house without Brenda?

KATE: I don't know.

KENNY: Fuck, what am I gonna say to Jennifer? What am I gonna tell the guys at the plant?

    What am I gonna say? What am I gonna do now? WHERE DO I EVEN START? TELL ME!

KATE: You should go to your buddy Will.

*(Beat.)*

KENNY: Right. That's fair.

*(More formal, rising.)*

I was wrong when I said Jennifer can't come here anymore. I hope you'll still let her. She's gonna need you, I think.

KATE: She's always welcome.

KENNY: *(As good-bye.)* I'm gonna go try to talk to my daughter.

*(Kenny goes to exit.)*

KATE: Kenny, Jennifer's here.

KENNY: She's here?

KATE: I can't bear to let you find her room empty too. She's upstairs with Matthew.

*(Permission.)*

Take your time.

KENNY: Thank you, Kate.

KATE: You're lucky I'm so damn OM.

(They smile. Kenny exits. Matthew enters.)

MATTHEW: HOLY CRAP! That was some serious shit that hit our fan!
I tried to turn up the stereo but she threatened to dump me.

KATE: We'll just let them be for a bit. Come. Sit here.

MATTHEW: Um. I'm starving. Can we bond tomorrow?

KATE: No.

(He sits.)

KATE: Do you have any questions about sex? About female genitalia?

MATTHEW: What? God, you're so embarrassing!

KATE: Are you having sex with Jennifer? Are you?

MATTHEW: What happened to "I know — I trust! — that Matthew isn't touching her."

KATE: Look me in the eyes and vow abstinence.

MATTHEW: Let's meditate.

KATE: Vow!

MATTHEW: I vow abstinence. OK? I love abstinence, I vow abstinence. Can I go make a sandwich now?

(Kate picks up the condoms.)

KATE: Yes.

(Beat.)

But I want you to put these in your wallet. To be prepared for an emergency.

MATTHEW: I've got my own.

KATE: Wait! What did you say?

MATTHEW: Nothing.

KATE: YOU HAVE YOUR OWN?

MATTHEW: 'Night Mom.

(Matthew exits.)

KATE: . . . Shit.


END OF PLAY

# Body Shop

ANNE PHELAN

This play was performed as part of the Twenty-Four Hour Play Festival at the William Inge Theatre Festival (Peter Ellenstein, Festival Director) in September 2003. It was directed by Hoite Caston.

## CHARACTERS

SAM: twenties

RACHEL: twenties; Sam's girlfriend, who owns the shop

MATT: twenties; a new customer with body image issues

STARR: twenties; customer who recently lost his sister


## SETTING/TIME

The play takes place in a body shop, in the very near future.

.　.　.

*Off left is the outside door, off right are the back office operations. Sam is sitting behind a desk. Phone rings. He picks it up.*

SAM: *(Into the phone.)* Body Shop, may I help you?

*(Listens.)*

I don't think so, let me check.

*(Rifles through papers on the desk.)*

I have no record of that. Are you sure you ordered it here?

*(Calling offstage.)*

Rachel!

RACHEL: *(Offstage.)* Yeah?

SAM: This guy says he placed an order for a small part?

RACHEL: *(Entering from off right.)* I haven't taken one in months.

SAM: Talk to him.

RACHEL: I'm busy.

SAM: But he wants to talk to you.

RACHEL: *(Grabs the phone from him. Into the phone.)* I have no time for stuff like that. Whatever.

*(Slams down the phone.)*

This is a body shop, not a Goddamn hardware store. We're weeks behind.

SAM: I do the best I can.

RACHEL: Well, you could start by not interrupting me with dumb customers with stupid questions. That's your job.

SAM: If it wasn't for me, we'd be the same low-rent, skanky store your mom started.

RACHEL: It was all my idea. You're the eye candy.

SAM: I am not! I'm a valuable asset.

RACHEL: You're the gatekeeper. Keep the damn gate. I can't do my job if you don't do yours.

SAM: Your mother wouldn't take that tone with me.

RACHEL: That's why Mom never could've handled the volume of business we do. She was too nice.

SAM: Hire more people, and stop driving me and yourself crazy.

RACHEL: Can't afford to. Suck it up.

SAM: Makes you mean.

RACHEL: You'd never say that if I was a man.

SAM: I wouldn't be sleeping with you if you were a man.

MATT: *(Enters from off left, carrying a head under his arm.)* I'd like some cosmetic work done.

SAM: Chest?

MATT: No, my head.

SAM: That's an expensive undertaking, sir. Parts, labor —

RACHEL: Overtime if it's a rush job —

SAM: I had my chest done last year. A little birthday gift to myself. Grandma always said to get yourself one gift, just in case you don't like what other people give you.

MATT: I have the part.

*(Puts the head on the desk.)*

RACHEL: *(Scrutinizes it.)* I have a better selection in the back —

SAM: It's a woman's head.

MATT: I know.

SAM: Why?

MATT: I got a good price on it. There was a close-out sale at the morgue —

RACHEL: Would you go to Ralph Lauren with fabric from K-mart and say, "Ralph, baby, whip this into a frock for me"? Our body work is art — just look at Sam. Or me.

*(She twirls for him.)*

I had my butt replaced last year.

SAM: *(Solemnly.)* A head is for a lifetime.

MATT: If that was true, I wouldn't be here.

RACHEL: I can't be turning out an inferior product. Word gets around. There are wars I have to supply — the Middle East, Liberia, Chechnya.

SAM: The whole India/Pakistan thing about Kashmir — that could blow anytime.

RACHEL: I need to preserve my reputation.

MATT: What if you did it, and I didn't tell anyone?

RACHEL: That sounds sleazy.

SAM: We are proud of our work. We give people a new lease on life. It shouldn't be turned into something tawdry.

MATT: But I always wanted to have eyes that color gray.

RACHEL: So buy contact lenses.

MATT: Never! That would be cheating.

SAM: You must have a better reason.

MATT: I hate my head — I always have. The way my eyebrows grow together, my funny earlobes —

STARR: *(Enters from off left, and lunges for the head.)* Who did this?
*(Matt grabs the head. They struggle with it.)*

MATT: It's mine! I bought it!

SAM: Don't you go spilling gray matter all over my sales room!

RACHEL: Break it up, guys.
*(She steps between them.)*

MATT: I paid $250 for that head.

RACHEL: You wuz robbed.

STARR: It's not for sale. It's mine!

MATT: Says who?

STARR: The coroner made a mistake. He gave me a note.

MATT: What, like when you're home sick in kindergarten and your mommy writes a note for the teacher? It's *my* head!

SAM: What do you think this is, some back-alley operation?

RACHEL: I don't churn out Frankensteins — you won't see Boris Karloff with a seam in his neck.

SAM: Actually, Boris Karloff was the monster. The doctor was Frankenstein. That's a common misconception.

RACHEL: Thanks, Roger Ebert, I'll remember that.

SAM: *(To Matt.)* Give him the ugly head and we'll give you a break on a show-room model.

STARR: It's not ugly! It's my sister.

MATT: I don't care if it's your mother! It's bought and paid for, and I've got a receipt.

SAM: Gentlemen, please.
*(To Matt.)*
Why don't you come with me, Mr. . . . ?

MATT: Hodges.

SAM: Mr. Hodges. I'll show you some of our inventory, and Ms. Hogwood can have a moment alone with him.

MATT: But I don't want to see anything —

SAM: Have you no intellectual curiosity, Mr. Hodges? That's what's wrong with this country — these days, no one can see any further than their own nose.

RACHEL: So true.

SAM: *(Motioning to Matt.)* Go ahead.

*(Matt exits off left. Sam gives Rachel a look as he follows him off.)*

STARR: *(Picks up the head.)* Thanks.

RACHEL: Where do you think you're going?

STARR: It's mine.

RACHEL: Even if it's not that Hodges guy's, he's got a receipt. And I've got heads back-ordered up the kazoo.

STARR: *(Holds the head up next to his face.)* Can't you see the familial resemblance?

RACHEL: Frankly, no. Let me look from here.

*(Crosses behind Starr. Slits his throat with a knife and he falls to the floor. Rachel looks him over.)*

Facial hair's always a plus with the Europeans.

SAM: *(Entering with a severed leg.)* He got away, honey pie. I'm sorry.

RACHEL: You got a foot. That's what matters. OK, let's dump these in the freezer and call it a day. What do you want for dinner?

SAM: I don't know why, but I'm in the mood for steak.

*(They exit, dragging off Starr's body.)*

END OF PLAY

# Perchance

## CRAIG POSPISIL

*Perchance* was produced by the 24 Hour Plays (Tina Fallon,
Kurt Gardner, Lindsay Bowen, and Philip Naude, producers)
at the Atlantic Theater in New York on May 7, 2005.
It was directed by Mark Lonergan, and the cast was
as follows: Robbie — Scott Wood;
Cass — Liz Elkins; Antonio — Matt Saldivar;
Cynthia/Ticket Agent/Gate Agent — Carla Rzeszewski.

## CHARACTERS
ROBBIE

CASS

ANTONIO

CYNTHIA/TICKET AGENT/GATE AGENT

## SETTING
A bare stage

· · ·

*The actors enter and take positions around the stage. Cass, Antonio, and Cynthia face away from the audience. Robbie, however, faces the audience.*

ROBBIE: It's kind of hazy, but what I remember is: Cass and I are in love. It's not perfect. I'm not going to lie and tell you that. But it was good, and I was happy. I didn't always know I was happy. In fact, sometimes I was downright miserable. And I don't just mean a little blue. I mean really depressed. And I'm not much fun to be around when I'm like that. I get pretty negative, call myself a failure. Things like that. I'm not suicidal or anything. Just depressed. A lot. Like everybody else, really. Just your average New Yorker, who was on Paxil for a while, but didn't like the sexual side effects, so tried Celexa, but that was worse, so then went on Wellbutrin for a couple years, and that was fine, but now is off the medication.
*(Slight pause.)*
Anyway Cass and I are in love. We live together. We've got a great life, good friends, terrific sex. Cass and me. With each other, not with the friends. As far as I know.
*(Slight pause.)*
Anyway, one morning —
*(Cass turns and faces inward, entering the scene.)*
CASS: I think I'm in love with someone else and I'm moving to San Diego.
ROBBIE: What?!
CASS: Robbie, it just isn't working between the two of us.
ROBBIE: How can you say that?
CASS: Because I think I'm in love with someone else, and I'm moving to San Diego.
ROBBIE: You can't be serious. When did this happen?

CASS: Well, I bought the plane ticket online last night.

ROBBIE: Last night?! You mean, before we went to Chez Josephine for our anniversary?

CASS: No, after that.

ROBBIE: We fell into bed and had sex right after dinner.

CASS: Yeah, it was after that too. I waited until you fell asleep, then I went online and got a really cheap ticket on Last Minute Travel.com. Then I called Antonio.

ROBBIE: Antonio?

CASS: He's this amazing guy I met at that publishing conference in Denver last month.

*(Antonio turns and faces the scene. He is suave and self-assured.)*

ANTONIO: Hello.

ROBBIE: Then she tells me about Denver.

*(Robbie steps back and watches the scene.)*

ANTONIO: You have the look of someone whose life has stagnated and who now longs for a fresh stream in which to swim.

CASS: Oh my God! How did you know?

ANTONIO: It is my gift. So, why does someone so beautiful look so sad?

CASS: I don't know if I can talk about this.

ANTONIO: Very well. I don't mean to intrude.

CASS: *(In a rush.)* You see, the thing is I've been living with my boyfriend, who I love, for four years, and things are great, . . . but they're exactly the same as they were at the beginning.

ANTONIO: And you long for change.

CASS: I don't know. Maybe. I mean, things are good. Sort of. Robbie can be a bit depressed sometimes and that gets old, believe me, but things are OK. It's just that things should change, right?

ANTONIO: Change is the essence of life. To deny change is to deny life itself.

CASS: Exactly. I mean, it's not like I'm one of those women who needs to be married, but after this much time shouldn't we be moving that way?

*(Robbie steps forward, addressing Cass.)*

ROBBIE: Wait! I've been thinking about asking you to marry me.

CASS: *(To Robbie.)* Well, how do I know that?

ANTONIO: I would marry you today.

CASS: What?

ROBBIE: You have *got* to be kidding me.

ANTONIO: You have to be bold when you feel a connection like this with another person. I have missed enough chances in my life to know I would rather take a chance than not.

CASS: *(To Robbie.)* I'm going to San Diego.

*(Cass and Antonio turns upstage. Robbie turns to the audience again.)*

ROBBIE: And she goes into the bedroom and starts packing. And I . . . I don't know what to do. My life's just exploded in my face and . . . and I leave. I walk out the door and just start walking. Until I find myself at my sister's home.

*(Cynthia, wearing a robe or dressing gown turns and faces Robbie.)*

CYNTHIA: The kids were a nightmare this morning. Brandie insisted she's going to school in her Cinderella costume from last Halloween, and Andrew couldn't find his English homework. And Joel didn't lift a finger to help me get the kids ready. I mean, I've got work to do too. Maybe it's not a nine-to-five job like Mr. Advertising, but I've got to turn on the computer and start tapping away. You want some coffee?

ROBBIE: Cass is leaving me.

CYNTHIA: Oh my God. What did you do?

ROBBIE: Me?!

CYNTHIA: Have you been ignoring her?

ROBBIE: No!

CYNTHIA: Have you been all, "Oh, I'm so depressed, and I'm such a failure. Why is everything in my life so terrible?"

ROBBIE: *(Unconvincingly.)* No.

CYNTHIA: Oh, Robbie. What are you going to do?

ROBBIE: What can I do? She's leaving me for this impulsive jerk, who asked her to marry him the same night he met her.

*(Slight pause.)*

What kills me is I went shopping for an engagement ring while she was in Denver. I was going to propose to her last night.

CYNTHIA: Why didn't you?

ROBBIE: I didn't find a ring I liked.

CYNTHIA: Oh, my God! If you wanted to propose, you should've just proposed! All right, look, if you want her, you've got to do some serious groveling. Where is she?

ROBBIE: On her way to Kennedy.

CYNTHIA: Then you better haul ass. And bring a gift. Something romantic.

*(Cynthia turns away. She ditches her robe and quickly ties a colorful scarf around her neck, morphing into a Ticket Agent, as Robbie faces the audience again.)*

ROBBIE: So I run out to go to the airport. I think about taking the A train, 'cause it's rush hour and I'm worried about traffic, but I spot a cab and flag it down.

*(Slight pause.)*

The ride takes forever and costs me sixty bucks but I finally get there. Her flight for San Diego leaves in fifteen minutes, but, of course I can't get to the gate without a ticket.

TICKET AGENT: Can I help you?

ROBBIE: I'd like a ticket please.

TICKET AGENT: *(Pause, waiting.)* . . . for what destination?

ROBBIE: Anywhere.

TICKET AGENT: I'm sorry. I don't understand, sir.

ROBBIE: What's your cheapest ticket to anywhere?

TICKET AGENT: I need a destination, sir.

ROBBIE: OK, how about Newark?

TICKET AGENT: Newark?

ROBBIE: Fine, ah, Washington. Is there a shuttle to Washington?

TICKET AGENT: Yes.

ROBBIE: Great. One ticket. One-way.

TICKET AGENT: One-way?

ROBBIE: Yeah, see I just need to get to one of the gates. I'm not really flying anywhere.

*(The Ticket Agent stares at him like he's insane or a terrorist or both.)*

ROBBIE: Kidding. I'm kidding. Make that round trip. And first-class.

*(The ticket agent turns away.)*

ROBBIE: Somehow I get through security in time.

*(Cass turns around. She carries a small overnight bag.)*

CASS: Robbie, what are you doing here?

ROBBIE: You can't go.

CASS: Don't do this.

ROBBIE: Please. I love you.

*(Antonio turns around and moves to Cass.)*

ANTONIO: My darling. I couldn't wait for your plane to arrive in San Diego, so I flew here overnight so we could begin our new adventure together right away.

ROBBIE: This cannot be happening.

ANTONIO: Who is this?

CASS: This is Robbie.

ANTONIO: *(Suppressing a laugh.)* Yes, I understand your desire for change.

*(Turning back to Cass.)*

I brought you a gift. This bottle is full of sand I found on the beaches of Ipanema. Some day I will take you there.

ROBBIE: Hey, I got you a gift too.

*(He takes a deck of playing cards out of his pocket. Cass takes them and looks at them, clearly unimpressed.)*

ROBBIE: It was all they had at the gift shop.

*(The Ticket Agent now turns back around as the Gate Agent.)*

GATE AGENT: Ladies and gentlemen, flight 574 for San Diego is ready for boarding. We will begin seating passengers in rows 20 and above.

ANTONIO: Shall we go?

CASS: I'm sorry, Robbie. I love you, but . . . I have to go.

ROBBIE: Marry me.

CASS: What?

ROBBIE: Marry me. I don't have a ring for you or a bottle of sand, but I love you and I want to spend my life with you. I just want to make you happy.

*(Antonio begins pulling Cass away, toward the Gate Agent and the door to the plane.)*

CASS: Robbie, I . . . .

GATE AGENT: Now, boarding all rows. Final boarding call.

ROBBIE: He doesn't love you. He doesn't know you. He doesn't know you like to sleep with that orange teddy bear or that you're always exactly ten minutes late to everything.

ANTONIO: *(To Cass.)* I know the real you.

*(Antonio leads Cass away, but she looks back. Robbie follows, handing his ticket to the Gate Agent.)*

GATE AGENT: Ticket please. This ticket is for Washington, D.C., sir.

ROBBIE: I just need to talk to her.

GATE AGENT: I'm sorry, sir. You can't get on this plane. Now, will you go, or do I have to call security?

ROBBIE: Cass! Please don't.

*(Robbie tries to get on the plane, but the Gate Agent wrestles him away from the door. Cass tries to move toward Robbie, but Antonio still pulls her away.)*

CASS: Robbie!

ROBBIE: Cass! Marry me!

CASS: Yes! Yes, I'll marry you!

*(Robbie and Cass reach for each other. The scene shifts into slow motion as*

*Robbie and Cass break free from the Gate Agent and Antonio, who are slowly spun away, before finally facing upstage in the original positions.)*
*(Robbie and Cass run toward each other. They do not touch, but spin around each other, somehow missing with Cass turning away, upstage to her original position, and Robbie coming back downstage to face the audience again.)*

ROBBIE: And then I woke up.

*(Slight pause.)*

It took me a minute, because I'd been in a deep sleep, and you know how it can take a while to get your bearings. What's real, what was the dream.

*(Slight pause.)*

But then I remember. I never went to the airport or tried to stop her. I never proposed. And she never came back.

*(The lights fade on Robbie.)*

END OF PLAY

# Triage
## An emergency for the stage in ten minutes

SHARYN ROTHSTEIN

*Triage* was originally produced by Youngblood at Ensemble Studio Theatre in New York, N.Y. in March, 2005. It was directed by Michael Kimmel. The cast was as follows:
Ronny — Cathy Curtin; Kenny — Gregg Mozgala;
Joe — William Jackson Harper; Sara — Jorelle Aronovitch.

CHARACTERS

    VERONICA (aka RONNY): a nurse

    KENNY: a nurse

    SARA: a choking woman, Caucasian

    JOE: Sara's fiancé, African-American

SETTING

    An emergency room

TIME

    The present

• • •

*An Emergency Room. Behind the counter sits Veronica and Kenny, nurses. They look at a client's paperwork and laugh. All of a sudden Joe, a black man, and his fiancée, Sara, a white woman, run into the room. Sara is choking.*

JOE: Excuse me! Excuse me!

RONNY: Next!

    *(Joe looks behind him. There is no one there.)*

JOE: Is that — ? Do you mean me?

RONNY: Are you Mr. Next?

JOE: No —

KENNY: Next left.

RONNY: Did he see a doctor?

KENNY: No.

RONNY: Did he see a nurse?

KENNY: No.

RONNY: Well did he see anybody?

KENNY: No.

RONNY: What was he suffering from?

KENNY: Temporary blindness.

    *(The nurses crack up.)*

JOE: Excuse me? I'm sorry — I think my fiancée is choking —

KENNY: Maybe you made her angry.

JOE: *(A little confused.)* She's not angry, she's choking.

RONNY: *(To Kenny.)* I'd be angry if I was choking.

JOE: She needs *help. (Looking around.)* I thought this was the Emergency Room.

KENNY: It *was* the Emergency Room.

JOE: What is it now?

RONNY: Oh it's back to being the Emergency Room. But last week it was having an identity crisis: It thought it was a living room.

*(Ronny and Kenny laugh.)*

JOE: What? Look, can you help my fiancée or not?

RONNY: We can admit her. But I don't know if we can help her. *(To Kenny.)* Can one person ever truly help another person?

JOE: But you're a doctor!

RONNY: *(Offended.)* I'm a nurse! I don't believe in doctors!

JOE: You don't believe in doctors??

RONNY: Not at all. In fact, I have very little faith in the medical profession as a whole.

JOE: *(Incredulous.)* Then why are you working at a hospital?

RONNY: I'm a nurse, where else would I work?

*(Sara throws herself on the floor.)*

KENNY: That looked painful.

JOE: I think she's allergic to lobster. *(Sad.)* I proposed tonight.

RONNY: Did she begin choking before or after you proposed?

JOE: After.

KENNY: And had she accepted your proposal?

JOE: Yes.

RONNY: And does she know that you're black?

JOE: *(Offended.)* What? Yes! Of course she does!

RONNY: And does it bother her?

JOE: No! It doesn't "bother" her that I'm black!

RONNY: *(To Kenny.)* 'Cause it would bother me.

JOE: We're in love. Love is colorblind!

KENNY: I had a dog who was color-blind.

JOE: *(Exasperated.)* All dogs are color-blind!

KENNY: Really? *(Beat.)* How is that relevant?

RONNY: If you want us to help her, you'll have to fill out these forms.

*(Kenny gives him a pile of forms.)*

And these

*(Kenny gives more.)*

And these and these and these.

JOE: *(Relieved.)* Fine, fine, thank you! *(To Sara.)* It's going to be OK, honey.

*(He looks at the form.)* Excuse me? I don't know her social security number.

KENNY: Uh oh.

*(Sara, on the floor, holds up her fingers to show her social security number, but Joe doesn't understand what she's doing.)*

RONNY: I thought you were her fiancée?

JOE: I am but we just got engaged not even an hour ago.

KENNY: You got engaged without knowing her social security number?

JOE: It didn't occur to me to ask.

RONNY: So you don't really know her at all, do you?

JOE: I know her, I just don't know her social security number.

KENNY: Do you know her birth sign?

JOE: Aquarius.

RONNY: Do you know her favorite food?

JOE: Meatballs.

KENNY: Do you know her brother?

JOE: She doesn't have a brother.

*(Ronny and Kenny shakes their heads, sadly.)*

RONNY: Yes. She does.

SARA: ("No I don't!") Nah mine donnnnnn.

KENNY: My God, she's forgotten her own brother.

*(Sarah begins choking more violently.)*

RONNY: *(Continued.)* What a drama queen.

JOE: Look, if you save her she can tell you her social security number herself.

RONNY: Well we can't save her without her social security number. I mean, what would we call her?

JOE: I promise I'll get her social security number before she leaves the hospital!

RONNY: Fine, fine. Fill out the rest of the paperwork and we'll help her.

JOE: Thank you. *(Returns to the papers.)* Wait — I don't understand — "What was Magellan's first name?" — Is this a quiz?

*(Ronny and Kenny throw confetti, dance a happy dance.)*

KENNY: POP QUIZ!!!

JOE: Why do I have to know Magellan's first name?

RONNY: To show you're well-educated.

JOE: Why do I have to be well-educated?

KENNY: Well you don't, but it certainly helps in today's job market.

JOE: No — no why do I have to be well-educated in order for my fiancée to see a doctor?

RONNY: Do you want the long answer or the short answer?

JOE: The short answer.

RONNY: Socioeconomics.

JOE: What's that?

KENNY: The short answer.

JOE: I always thought Magellan was his first name.

*(Kenny and Ronny scoff.)*

KENNY: As if!

SARA: ("Ferdinand.") Ferrnnnn

JOE: What's that honey?

SARA: FERDINAND!

JOE: Oh Ferdinand! That's his first name! *(To Sara.)* You're so smart, baby, that's why I love you. *(Sara chokes, Joe speaks in baby talk.)* Yes, yes I do love you —

RONNY: *(Disappointed, rolling her eyes.)* Alright. Just tell us her insurance company and we'll admit her.

JOE: Her insurance company?

KENNY: She is insured isn't she?

JOE: Sure. I'm sure she's insured. I'm sure of it.

RONNY: That sounded repetitive.

KENNY: So what's her insurance?

JOE: I — I don't know —

RONNY: But you're sure she's insured?

JOE: Yes.

RONNY: Now see if I could bet on it —

KENNY: — we're not allowed to bet on the patients . . . *technically* —

RONNY: — I'd be betting that she's not insured. You know why? Nobody's insured. Most people spend their lives praying they don't get run over by a possessed bus driver or stomped on by a diabolical stegadon.

JOE: A stegadon?

RONNY: Yes, a prehistoric dwarf elephant.

JOE: But if it's a dwarf elephant, why do you care if it steps on you?

KENNY: Because it would still hurt. God. You really don't know anything about prehistoric elephants do you?

JOE: I don't care about prehistoric elephants! I care about my fiancée! She's going to die.

RONNY: Well she might as well die. She's couldn't afford to live after all the tests we'd put her through. Did you know that a pregnancy test in the ER costs $125?

JOE: She's not pregnant! We haven't even had sex yet. She's a virgin!

*(Sara shoots Joe a look for telling them she's a virgin.)*

KENNY: Really? She doesn't look like a virgin.

JOE: What does that mean?

KENNY: She looks a little slutty to me, throwing her body around like that.

JOE: She's choking!

RONNY: Choking is no excuse for promiscuity.

JOE: Look — she doesn't need a pregnancy test, all she needs is the Heimlich Maneuver.

RONNY: Whose maneuver?

KENNY: Heimlich. *(Beat, to Joe.)* Who's Heimlich?

JOE: You don't know the Heimlich Maneuver?

RONNY: Is it a method for stuffing sausages?

JOE: No!

KENNY: Does it involve excessive shoe horning?

JOE: No!

RONNY: Then why would we have heard of it?

JOE: Because you're a nurse! *(Looks around wildly.)* My God, is there anyone here who can save her?

KENNY: Well, I guess I can try. *(He stands behind Sara in Heimlich position.)* Has she accepted Jesus as her Lord and Savior?

JOE: She's Jewish!

KENNY: Oh. *(He drops her on the ground.)* Well that explains why she's choking.

JOE: You think she's choking because she's Jewish?

RONNY: Well she's certainly not darning a yarmulke.

JOE: No, she's choking! She's been choking for the last half hour!

KENNY: And she's still alive? That's amazing!

JOE: Well she's not going to be alive for much longer if you don't help her!

RONNY: We obviously can't help her she's not insured. However, you can certainly try to save her.

JOE: I can?

KENNY: Sure. Just don't break her sternum.

JOE: What happens if I break her sternum?

RONNY: She dies. *(Laughs.)* Just kidding! *(Dead serious.)* No really. She dies.

JOE: Oh God. I don't know what to do.

SARA: SAVE ME YOU MORON!

JOE: Oh. OK. Here goes.

*(He gets in a position to save her. He takes a deep breath and pushes down on her chest.)*

JOE: Arghh!

*(Sara coughs, she gurgles, she giggles, she coughs, she dies.)*

JOE: What — wait — what happened?

RONNY: *(Sadly.)* You broke her sternum.

JOE: What? I did? I broke her sternum? I killed her? Are you saying I killed her?

KENNY: That's what we're saying.

JOE: I killed my fiancée? My one true love?! My platypus face? I killed her??

RONNY: Yes, you killed her. But you did it in our hospital, so we're going to have charge you for it.

*(Kenny gives Joe a bill.)*

JOE: What?

KENNY: Good medical care is expensive these days.

JOE: But we didn't receive good medical care!

RONNY: Bad medical care is expensive too.

JOE: But — But — She didn't have to die. She didn't have to die!

RONNY: Of course she did. *(Simply.)* She didn't have health insurance.

*(Ronny and Kenny return to their paperwork. Joe stares at the bill. Sara's body twitches on the floor.)*

END OF PLAY

# Dog Lovers

S. W. SENEK

This play was originally produced by the Manhattan Comedy Collective in N.Y.C. in 2006. It was directed by Anthony Luciano. The cast was as follows: Missy — Kristi Funk; Mitsy — Samara Doucette; Pete — Blake White; Peekar — Matt Bridges. This play was also performed at the 2006 New York Fifteen Minute Play Festival at the American Globe Theatre. It was directed by Anthony Luciano. The cast was as follows: Missy — Stacy Mayer; Mitsy — Sandra Holguin; Pete — Blake White; Peekar — Joel Stigliano.

CHARACTERS

MISSY

PETE

MITSY (a dog)

PEEKAR (a dog)

SETTING

A bare stage

• • •

MISSY: *(To the audience.)* For the last six months, I have been lonely.

MITSY: *(To the audience.)* Very lonely — it's pathetic.

MISSY: I'm in search of, well, a man. However, not just *any* man.

MITSY: She has her needs.

MISSY: I'm a very finicky fitness instructor — like my muscles, I have limits. You see in my past relationships, "he" always wanted "me" to give up the things I love most: sit-ups after eating *Godiva* Chocolates, listening to the hum of air conditioners, and my little poodle, Mitsy.

MITSY: That's me.

MISSY: That's her. My beautiful Mitsy. So, any man who wants me, has to want Mitsy — we're a package — all or nothing at all. I mean, the last guy I dated, he was allergic to dogs.

MITSY: It's rude when someone's allergic to you.

MISSY: "It's either me or the dog," he said.

MITSY: He gave her one minute and thirty-three seconds.

MISSY: Give my up little girl? Never! No!

MITSY: Then he sneezed on me.

MISSY: He sneezed and left.

MITSY: Missy is so good to me. She gives me exercise, feeds me, rubs my belly, scoops up my feces from the sidewalk and parades it in a baggy. I say anyone who proudly does that, well, they're special.

MISSY: I enjoy doing the little things for her. Together, *we're* beautiful.

MITSY: Besides my dream of being in a movie — there's no place I'd rather be.

MISSY: Sometimes I sense that she'd like to be in a movie. I hope I'm not holding her back.

MITSY: *(To Missy.)* Surely you're not.

MISSY: *(To Mitsy.)* Good. *(Beat. Aside.)* It's so weird, on occasion — it's like I can hear her talk to me. But that's silly, dogs can't talk, right? Right. *(Beat.)* So a friend of mine suggests, "Why don't you find your perfect man online — another dog lover." Well, I never tried that before. So, I reluctantly sign up on Desperatedates.com; write my blurb — with the perfect heading: "You can't exercise Missy without exercising Mitsy." *(Look of question. She's not sure if the heading makes sense.)* To top it off, I find a perfect picture to post. *(They pose.)* Then? I wait —

MITSY: Wait —

MISSY: And wait. Finally, I get a reply — the subject reads: "Dog Lovers at Madison Park."

MITSY: And attached is a picture. *(Pete and Peekar pose. Sound: Bing.)*

MISSY: Pete —

MITSY: And Peekar. *(They both sigh.)*

MISSY: His profile is amazing. It mirrors mine — *he* is also a fitness instruc-tor. Wow. So we e-mail back and forth and in a blink of an eye, we set up a time to meet at Madison Park. Who knows, right? Right.

MITSY: We go to the park to meet. Then —

*(At the park. Pete and Peekar still pose while waiting on a park bench.)*

PETE: *(Out of his pose.)* Missy? Mitsy? Is that you?

MISSY AND MITSY: *(Missy and Mitsy do a quick pose of their picture online.)* It's us! *(Sound: Bing.)*

PETE: Look Peekar, it's Mitsy. You see? She's — they're picturesque — just like the picture.

MISSY: And your picture — adorable.

PETE: I'm Pete — this is Peekar. *(Pete and Peekar quick pose again. Sound: Bing.)* I'm sorry if I seem excited, it's — well, it's just been countless dates of — *(Pete crosses closer to Missy.)* well, you see, when you replied with a picture of you and Mitsy, I knew it was right, I could feel it. *(He discretely breathes in Missy's scent.)* Go on buddy, say hi.

PEEKAR: *(To Mitsy.)* Hi. I'm Peekar . . . I'm a dog. I eat dog food that's for sen-sitive stomachs.

MITSY: *(To Peekar.)* Hi. I'm Mitsy . . . I like to pee-pee on that tree over there.

MISSY: *(To the audience.)* Our first "date" is so refreshing. We talk about exer-cise machines, the New York City telephone directory, monthly enemas —

PETE: *(To Missy.)* I don't go anywhere without Peekar. He's my world.

MISSY: *(To Pete.)* And Mitsy's *my* world.

MITSY: *(To the audience.)* It takes thirteen minutes for Peekar to feel comfort-able, but when he does —

PEEKAR: *(To Mitsy.)* I know we just met —

MITSY: *(To Peekar.)* Yes?

PEEKAR: But —

MITSY: Yes?

PEEKAR: You want to smell my back end?

MITSY: One sniff wouldn't hurt — to know who you are of course.

PEEKAR: Of course.

    *(Peekar turns around, prepares — Mitsy prepares, then proceeds.)*

MISSY: *(To the audience.)* We hit it off. Finally, a man who has a parallel understanding.

MITSY: *(To the audience.)* Peekar is different then those other dogs, he's charming — and honest — in a dog-kind of way.

MISSY: So we set up another date.

PETE: *(Hands a picture of a paw print to Missy.)* For you and Mitsy. Peekar made it.

MITSY: *(To the audience.)* He's an artist.

PEEKAR: I call it *Paw*.

MITSY: *(To the audience.)* He likes me for more than just my body. He sees me for my intellect.

MISSY: And Pete and I are — well, there's something about him. *(Pete and Missy exchange an intense look.)* And I likey.

MITSY: All I can think about is the park and Peekar's back end.

MISSY: All I can think about is kissing Pete. But that means we'd have to get to date number three? Does he even like me? Suddenly, he calls and says — "Us, the *dogs*, noon, at —

MISSY AND PETE: The park.

MISSY: How sweet is this — Pete has another gift for me — well, for Mitsy.

MITSY: What is it? Tell me!

PETE: *(At the Park.)* I couldn't control myself, I was at the pet store this morning, and what do I see?

MISSY: Oh, you didn't have to —

PETE: Well, actually I didn't.

MISSY: You didn't?

PETE: *Peekar* did! *(Pete enthusiastically laughs then reveals the toy.)*

MITSY: *(To Peekar.)* A fire hydrant squeaker toy. I've always wanted one. That was so sweet of you. Peekar.

PEEKAR: I got it because I think you're real special. It reminds me of you — when you pee-pee. It's like, when you're ready to go — you open her up and WOOSH! *(He squeaks the toy. Mitsy flops around.)*

MITSY: Oh, Peekar! *(Squeaks toy.)*

MISSY: Look, she's excited.

MITSY: This makes me very excited. *(She squeaks the toy.)*

PEEKAR: You being excited makes *me* very excited!

PETE: Look how excited they are. This is exciting!

MITSY: I can't contain myself — *(She gives Peekar a kiss.)*

PEEKAR: Wow! A kiss!

PETE: She kissed him. She kissed him! Way to go Peekar!!

MISSY: *(Staring at Pete.)* They're really bonding.

PETE: This moment makes me proud.

MISSY: Thank you for the gift — that was so sweet of you — and Peekar. *(Beat. Missy grabs Pete and kisses him.)*

PEEKAR: Wow! She kissed Pete!

MITSY: She kissed him! All this kissing — I want to kiss you again! *(Mitsy grabs Peekar and kisses him again. This time longer.)*

PETE: Now look at them! Go on Peekar! Yes! Yes! *(Pete jumps up and down in excitement. Missy grabs Pete and kisses him longer. Pete, while kissing Missy, tries to sneak a peak at Mitsy and Peekar.)* Go get her!

MITSY: *(To the audience.)* It is *so* clear —

MISSY: In so little time — *(To Mitsy.)* Mitsy, I'm in love.

MITSY: *(To Missy.)* Missy, *I'm* in love.

MISSY: *(To the audience.)* The way Pete gets animated about Mitsy and Peekar — it's incredible. Just yesterday, before we parted, Pete says to me —

PETE: This is really working out — the dogs and me — us.

MISSY: And it keeps getting better. Countless dates at the park. Mitsy continues to get showered with gifts: *(Pete and Peekar hand Missy and Mitsy various gifts. During this, there is showroom music.)* grooming gift certificates *(Pete hands Missy an oversized gift certificate.)*, treats *(Pete hands Missy large treats. Missy stuffs one in Mitsy's mouth.)*, and a *bodacious blue bow! (Pete hands Missy the large bow. Missy places the bow on Mitsy.)*

MITSY: *(To the audience.)* Peekar and I have so much in common — we're both dogs, and we bark!

MISSY: Weeks pass. More paintings *(Pete hands Missy an armful of paintings.)* — and gifts! *(Pete enters with a large, cartoon-looking, high stack of wrapped presents. Music ends.)*

PEEKAR: *(Sitting with Mitsy looking at a painting.)* This painting was inspired by your outer beauty. I call it "the other paw."

MISSY: Before my eyes, Peekar and Mitsy become more intimate. I start to feel — well —

MITSY: *(At the park.)* Peekar, I'd watch it. I'm in heat. I'm liable to hump your head — and I don't care who sees.

PEEKAR: That's a sign Mitsy — that we're ready to open our relationship up to the whole world.

MITSY: Really?

PEEKAR: Really!

MITSY: *(Howling.)* YES!!

PEEKAR: *(Howling.)* YES!!!

*(Mitsy gets on top of Peekar.)*

MISSY: Mitsy, should you be doing that to Peekar? Mitsy? *(To Pete.)* Should they really be doing this?

PETE: It must be true love — Go on Peekar! Way to take it! Way to take it!

MISSY: *(To the audience.)* I've never seen a man get excited about one dog humping another one's head — but he's a dog lover and so am I. Right? Right.

MITSY: *(To the audience.)* Peekar and me, our relationship is flowering — moving forward. Talking about fleas, puking up grass — we're becoming *serious*.

MISSY: Pete and I are — well, we're not moving forward. All of our — well, *his* attention has been on the dogs.

PETE: *(At the park. Pete is taking pictures of Peekar and Missy playing.)* Would you look at them . . . *(Proud smile.)*

MISSY: Pete, how long have we been together.

PETE: Well, let's see, Mitsy and Peekar have been dating oh, I'd say three months.

MISSY: Three months?

PETE: Yes, we've — *they've* been "together" for three months. Aren't they just priceless?

MISSY: How come our conversation never moves past dogs and the new elliptical machines at the fitness center?

PETE: *(Ignoring her.)* This picture's perfect — I'm going to hang it next to my elliptical machine.

PEEKAR: *(To Mitsy. They are lying next to each other.)* This is the life, isn't it, strategically placed here in the shade. You know, you're all I think about when I can remember things.

MITSY: Oh, Peekar.

PEEKAR: Oh, such a beautiful summer's day to be with the one you care about.

MITSY: *(To Missy.)* Do you hear that? He said "one" — I'm the "one."

MISSY: *(To the audience.)* I thought *I* was the "one."

MITSY: *(To the audience.)* I slowly start to detect a jealousy in Missy.

*(At the park. Pete is playing in between the dogs.)*

PETE: My handsome Peekar, and *beautiful* Mitsy. You are a perfect match — yes you are *(Makes a face like he's talking to a baby.)* Yes, you are. *(Laughs and looks at Missy.)* Aren't they?

MISSY: Pete, is there something wrong with me?

PETE: What's the problem, Missy?

MISSY: You've hardly spoken to me the whole day — instead you're collecting kisses from Mitsy and Peekar. Wouldn't you rather have kisses from me?

PETE: Gee, there's no reason to be jealous. You could join in. Don't you know love when you see it? *(Putting his head between Mitsy and Peekar.)*

MISSY: Of course I do, it's just I want to make sure you love me for me. *(Pete gets his camera out.)*

PETE: Missy, you are special. I mean, look at us — and them! *(Out of the corner of his eye, he sees Peekar and Mitsy cuddling.)* Oh my God! I have to get this picture — they are adorable!

MITSY: Would you be here if I wasn't beautiful?

PEEKAR: *(To Mitsy.)* Of course I would —

MITSY: Really.

PEEKAR: Really . . . you know, I think we're in love.

MITSY: *(Back at home. To Missy.)* Hurray!! "We're" in love! He said "we're" in love! Do you hear that Missy!? Missy?

MISSY: *(To the audience.)* What about me?

MITSY: Love!

MISSY: *I* want a little attention — so I decide to meet Pete at the park without Mitsy.

MITSY: *(Calling out.)* Missy — where are you? Missy? Why am I locked in the bathroom?

PETE: *(At the Park. Pete and Peekar look puzzled because Mitsy isn't there.)* Hey, ah, Missy . . . where's Mitsy?

MISSY: She's at home, she's under the weather . . . You know, the doggy runs.

PEEKAR AND PETE: Ew.

MISSY: All over the priceless bear rug.

PETE: My God, why didn't you call? Peekar and I could have brought nutritional food to her. This is really selfish of you. Wait — who's watching *her?* She could be dead. *(Almost speechless.)* I can't even face you right now. *(He turns away and covers Peekar's eyes.)* You must return to your place, take care of Mitsy — I beg of you! Don't contact me until she's healed. Meanwhile, Peekar and I will go home, light candles, and pray for Mitsy's safe recovery.

MITSY: *(At Missy's apartment.)* Missy? Where are you?!

MISSY: *(To Mitsy.)* You!

MITSY: *(To Missy.)* Me?

MISSY: Yes, you!

MITSY: You can hear what I'm saying?

MISSY: You're sabotaging my romance! Traitor!

MITSY: Why are you doing this to me? Why are you keeping me away from Peekar and Pete?

MISSY: "Peekar and Pete" — Peekar and Pete! What ever happened to "I love only *you*, Missy."

MITSY: Just because Peekar loves me — jealousy only leads to rage!

MISSY: He loves you so much, huh? Well, slowly, I'll give them the new Mitsy — we'll see if they still want you. *(She roughly removes the bow from Mitsy.)*

MITSY: My bodacious blue bow!

PETE: *(At the park.)* Her bodacious blue bow — the one we bestowed upon her, what happened to it?

MISSY: I'm afraid . . . she ate it. *(Presents chewed bow. Pete and Peekar gasp.)*

PETE: That's not like you, Mitsy.

PEEKAR: *(To Mitsy.)* Say it isn't so.

MITSY: Peekar, it's a lie! I didn't chew it.

MISSY: Peekar, I wouldn't listen to Mitsy — she's been telling a lot of fibs . . . perhaps it's the medication.

PEEKAR AND PETE: Medication?

MISSY: She has a slight chemical imbalance . . . according to our very intelligent vet.

PEEKAR: Mitsy?

MITSY: It's not true, Peekar! Don't believe her — you're my only hope — it's not true —

MISSY: *(Stroking Mitsy.)* Now, now, Mitsy — easy girl — perhaps we should leave now. *(To Pete.)* I'll call you tomorrow, sweetheart. *(Kisses Pete on the cheek.)*

MITSY: *(Back at home.)* You're ruining my life!

MISSY: *(To the audience.)* Then I decide not to walk her as much —

PETE: *(At the park.)* Is she gaining weight?

MISSY: At least ten pounds.

PETE AND PEEKAR: Ten?

MISSY: It's her bad hip.

*(Peekar and Pete gasp.)*

MITSY: *(Crosses to Peekar.)* Please help me Peekar.

PEEKAR: You're breath stinks, Mitsy.

MISSY: *(To the audience.)* And the grooming? Well, I keep forgetting — one appointment after another and . . . *(Messes up Mitsy's hair.)*

MITSY: *(To Missy.)* My hair — anything but my hair! You use to love grooming me!

MISSY: *(To Mitsy.)* That was before you betrayed me!

PETE: *(At the park.)* My God! What's happened to her!

MISSY: The imbalance is worse than we thought. She snaps without warning. I wouldn't stand too close.

MITSY: *(Snaps at Peekar.)* How can you believe her! *(Pete and Peekar back off.)* She's full of lies!

PETE: Watch it Peekar — Our Mitsy's miffed. She's dangerous!

MITSY: I'm not dangerous! You must believe me Peekar! I love you!

MISSY: Beware of her deceptiveness, Peekar! She realizes not what she says! She's taking nonprescribed drugs — they're altering her into some kind of monster!

MITSY: Don't listen to her!

MISSY: She barely obeys me anymore.

PEEKAR: What's happened — you've let yourself go! You're not beautiful anymore . . . — you're not the Mitsy I met. You're a — a monster! I don't love you anymore!

MITSY: How can you be so shallow! I thought you loved me for who I am!

PEEKAR: No, I loved you for who you were —

MITSY: I'm still me!

PEEKAR: There's too much of you!

MITSY: No!

PEEKAR: *(Howling.)* YES!

MITSY: *(Howling.)* NO!

*(Peekar turns his back on Mitsy.)*

PETE: Peekar — what's happened to our Mitsy? She has become tainted.

MISSY: You still have me.

PETE: But look at *her*. I spent months searching for the perfect dog. *She* was the chosen "one."

MISSY: What about us? Or was there ever an "us"?

PETE: I'm sorry Missy, but —

MISSY: I knew it. It was never about me, was it?

PETE: It's more complex than that.

MISSY: It's true. You only loved me for my dog —

PETE: It was the only way Missy, can't you see — I wanted to find a nice dog that I — Peekar could kiss. For me — him to share all our dark little secrets. For me — him to mate with. He's my best friend. You of all people should understand. We're dog lovers, right? *(Beat.)* Look — forget Mitsy — we could research "together" — purchase another dog. We'll start over. *(Extends his hand.)* Join us.

MISSY: I'm sorry Pete, I'm just not into pets the way you are. *(Hands the squeaker toy back to Pete. A moment.)*

PETE: You're like the rest of them, limited. We could have been something — all four of us. *(Beat.)* Let's go home Peekar.

PEEKAR: I think this will be the start of my dark period as an artist.

PETE: *(To Peekar.)* You know sometimes, I can hear you perfectly. *(He draws in closer to Peekar — practically ready to kiss him, but Peekar's paw stops him.)* Come Peekar. Let's go look at show-dog magazines. So long Missy. *(They exit.)*

*(Long pause.)*

MISSY: *(To Mitsy.)* That whole experience was kind of weird, huh?

MITSY: *(To Missy.)* It was horrible — how can things ever be the same? *(Beat.)* I've decided to run away from you.

MISSY: *(To Mitsy.)* I'm sorry Mitsy — I never meant to hurt you.

MITSY: I know . . . but I'm still running away.

MISSY: OK . . . ?

MITSY: Well, bye.

MISSY: Bye.

MITSY: *(To the audience.)* A year has passed. What a terrific journey life has brought since the whole New York thing. When I left Missy, I ran and ran and ran and didn't stop — except to tinkle. For the first time, I was free. Talk about seeing the country. I made it all the way to California — like the Joads in the *Grapes of Wrath* — traveling across the country gave me time to read. Suddenly, without warning, I'm captured and placed in a rescue shelter — but who picks me up? Mr. Hollywood director . . . and *I'm* his only girl. Me. He's so sweet. *(Smiles.)* Oh, my dreams have been fulfilled — he's used me in a few of his movies. I'm in movies! A star! Of course, he's — *we're* now sick of Hollywood — and he wants to move back to New York — to do theater . . . New York. Sometimes, you have to go back to your roots — makes you stronger. *(Takes in a deep breath.)* I miss the parks . . .

MISSY: *(To the audience.)* My dating life — like my abs, is fantastic. No more obstacles — just one date after another after another. Although, I must admit, I still use the picture of Mitsy and me for my online dating profile. I get tons of questions about the dog. I tell them doggy no more — she died. *(Laugh.)* It really gets them. As for dating guys with dogs? I don't mind. I now know the only thing I have to offer is me. *(Beat.)* I still hold out hope that someday I'll meet the "one." Oh, today my friend e-mailed me about *her* friend who's moving to New York — says he's cute and available — a Hollywood film director — who now wants to do theater . . . apparently, he has a dog. *(Big sigh.)* I just love dogs.

END OF PLAY

# The Agenda

PAUL SIEFKEN

*The Agenda* by Paul Siefken was originally commissioned and produced for *Revenge* by: The Drilling Company, artistic director Hamilton Clancy. It was presented at 78th Street Theatre Lab in New York City, June 3, 2005. It was directed by Tom Demenkoff, stage managed by Billie Davis with sets by Paul Gelinas, lights by Dans Sheehan, original live music by Tom Garvey with the following cast: Tim — Mike Dressel; Peter — Ben Masur; Jerry — Douglas Taurel; John — Eirik Gislasson.

## CHARACTERS

TIM: a young, fit man in his early twenties.

PETER: a well-dressed professional, mid-thirties. Smug. He's used to calling the shots.

JOHN: a large, muscular man about thirty. Quietly threatening but surprisingly articulate when he opens his mouth

JERRY: a lean, muscular man about thirty, also threatening-looking, but
his speech is softer than John's. John and Jerry are a team.

## SETTING

A small apartment

. . .

*Setting: A small apartment, stylishly minimalist furnishings. A single large
framed black-and-white photograph of two men, Tim and Peter, hangs on
the wall. Several suitcases are gathered near the door. A tense silence fills the
room.*

*At Rise: Peter stands near the door. He's clearly preparing to leave. Tim
stands several feet away running his fingers through his hair in frustration.
They've been arguing for some time. Peter grabs for his suitcases. Exasperated,
Tim tries one more time to get Peter to stay.*

TIM: I just don't understand.

PETER: No. I wouldn't expect you to.

TIM: It's just that, I thought everything was fine. Not just fine . . . great.

PETER: I know.

TIM: So what happened? Why are you doing this to me?

PETER: It's not about you.

TIM: Oh, please. Did you really just say that? After six months together? I
think I deserve better than the "It's not you, it's me" routine!

PETER: I didn't say that. I said it's not *about* you. It's not *about* me either.

TIM: Then who is it about, Peter?

PETER: Trust me, Tim, you don't want to have this conversation. Not now.
You'll understand soon.

TIM: What the hell does that mean? Look, is it someone else? If it is, just tell
me!

PETER: That would make it so much easier, wouldn't it?

TIM: Yes, Peter, it would. At least then I'd have a reason why!

PETER: You want to know why? Because. That's why.

TIM: Since when did you become such a sarcastic asshole?

*(Peter shrugs.)*

TIM: Well it's not like you. You're not *cold* like this.

PETER: You have no idea what I'm really like.

TIM: Bullshit. You don't spend this much time with someone, share a life with them, share a bed with them, without knowing who they are.

PETER: I guess *you* do.

TIM: Stop it, Peter. God! This doesn't make any sense! You said you loved me. Just yesterday! You said it yesterday, for Christ's sake! And now I come home and you've packed up all your shit! This is fucked up, Peter!

PETER: Sorry, Tim, things change. And I'm afraid this is the real me. This is how I work.

TIM: I don't accept that.

PETER: And that's too bad. But there's nothing more to say. I really have to go.

*(Tim reaches and grabs Peter's arm.)*

TIM: No! No! You're not walking out on me like this.

PETER: Get off of me, you stupid fag.

*(Tim releases Peter and takes a step back.)*

TIM: What did you just say?

PETER: *(Sighs.)* You're stupid, Tim. That's why we picked you.

TIM: Who's we? Who picked me? What's going on here, Peter?

PETER: Good-bye Tim.

*(Peter tries to leave again, but Tim, suddenly furious, grabs him forcefully and pushes him against the wall.)*

TIM: Answer me!

PETER: Jerry? John? A little help?

*(Jerry and John enter the room from the main door. They pull Tim off Peter, Tim struggles, they release him, and stand on either side of him silently with their arms folded facing Peter. Peter straightens his clothes.)*

PETER: Thanks, guys.

*(Tim looks at both and then he leans toward Peter.)*

TIM: *(Quietly.)* Peter? Who the hell are these guys?

PETER: Tim, meet Jerry and John.

*(Tim looks back and nods at each.)*

TIM: Now, do you mind telling me what the fuck they were doing outside our apartment!

PETER: As a precaution. In case you freaked out. Which you did.

TIM: Sure, that makes sense. Two huge bodyguards attack me out of nowhere. That will keep me from freaking out!

PETER: They're not bodyguards. They're friends. Brothers really.

*(Jerry and John hold up their fists in solidarity. Seeing this, Tim leans toward Peter again.)*

TIM: Jesus, Peter. Are you in some kind of cult?

PETER: We prefer to call it a movement.

TIM: A movement. To do what?

JERRY/JOHN: *(In unison.)* To free the gay people from the oppression of the straight man.

TIM: This is a joke, right?

PETER: No joke.

*(Tim sees that no one is smiling.)*

TIM: And you're leaving me because of this movement?

PETER: Yes. Like I said, we picked you.

TIM: To leave? To hurt? Why? What kind of threat am I to you? In case you hadn't noticed, I'm gay!

PETER: You are now.

TIM: Now? What is that supposed to mean? I've always been gay. Since as far back as I can remember. Since . . .

PETER: Since high school?

*(Tim looks surprised.)*

PETER: Since Jeremy Shaw from your wrestling team? Tim?

TIM: Yes.

PETER: He was your partner.

TIM: My wrestling partner.

PETER: And he taught you a few special moves, didn't he?

TIM: How do you know that? I never told you . . .

PETER: You didn't need to. Jeremy was our idea. He's one of our best field operatives.

TIM: Field operatives! It was high school!

PETER: We've found that's the best place to make the initial contact.

TIM: You actually expect me to believe that Jeremy was some kind of top-secret queer high school hustler that you sent to seduce me and turn me gay?

PETER: Bingo.

TIM: That's insane!

PETER: Not really. Think about it, Tim. Why would we target you, specifically? What possible leverage would our movement gain from making you, Tim Hatcher, gay?

*(Tim considers this a moment.)*

TIM: Does this have something to do with my father?

PETER: The good congressman? I think you're on to something. Take it for a spin and see how it rides.

TIM: You had my high school wrestling partner seduce me six years ago and have been setting me up with partners ever since, including you Peter, all so you could embarrass my father?

*(Peter touches his nose — on the nose.)*

TIM: That's preposterous!

PETER: No, I'd say it's your father's worst nightmare. That all the venom he's been spitting about the gay agenda up there on Capitol Hill is actually true. His fears validated. His warnings justified. There really is a conspiracy to corrupt the innocent youth of America and turn them down the dark and "sinful" path of homosexuality, Congressman Hatcher. And guess what? We sodomized your son.

*(Peter puts his arm around Tim.)*

PETER: But look at it this way, Timmy, at least you know that your father's not some paranoid crazy man. Think of it as the ultimate self-fulfilling prophecy.

TIM: But he doesn't even know I'm gay.

PETER: He does now. And so does the press.

TIM: No! Please no. Tell me you didn't.

PETER: Sorry, Tim.

TIM: You've destroyed my life. My father's life. All to make a point?

PETER: Don't flatter yourself, Tim. You and your father are just the tip of the iceberg.

TIM: There are others? How many? How long has this been going on?

PETER: *(Sighs.)* John? Jerry? Give him the presentation.

*(John and Jerry step forward. John removes the picture from the back wall of the apartment. Peter hands Jerry a briefcase. Jerry opens the briefcase and takes out a projector. He lights up the now bare wall with the projector. John begins addressing both Tim and the audience, while Jerry advances slides with a remote control. Tim is completely baffled at first but eventually becomes engrossed in the presentation. Nothing ever actually appears in the slide show.)*

JOHN: America has a long history of abusing, neglecting, and otherwise ignoring its gay men and women. But in the twentieth century, we began to emerge from our collective closet. A gay culture began to take hold, almost exclusively in liberal big cities like New York and San Francisco. And the straight man seemed to accept this new development as long as we stayed isolated on our little urban islands of homosexuality. But it was from these islands that our talents transcended our place in society. Soon, we were known as a dominating cultural force in the art, fashion, and entertainment industries, through which the straight man feared our lifestyle might be promoted. In the 1980s, a covert war was waged against gay America, right under the nose, or possibly the watchful eye, of Ronald Reagan, an actor no less. And some feared this secret war included the government's secret manufacturing of AIDS as a disease meant to eradicate our people. It was around this time that our leader decided to take a stand.

*(At this point, Jerry turns off the projector and Peter pulls a large book from his bags. He brings it to John, who holds the book open like a big picture book, turning pages as Jerry continues the history lesson. The pages are blank.)*

JERRY: Our founder, Michael, was standing outside of a gay bar when he was approached by two straight men. They began to taunt him with the usual gay slurs. Michael had seen a lot of sickness and death at that point. He was left with nothing but anger. And he just snapped. He beat the two men within an inch of their lives, and left them broken and bleeding on the sidewalk. It was then that he had a revelation. There was no need to be afraid of the straight man. The most hateful among them were fat, weak, and stupid. If they wanted a reason to fear homosexuals, he would give them one. He began recruiting in gay gyms. It was not hard to find an eager and willing army of well-toned young men to start his secret revolution. Together, they began a campaign of violence, beating straight men to a pulp in back alleys, knowing the incidents would never be reported by their ridiculously macho victims. This underground movement spread across the country, and as a tribute to another revolutionary group, they came to be known as "The Pink Panthers."

*(John puts down the book and slowly walks to the front of the stage as he takes over the presentation. Jerry produces a letter from his pocket and reacts dramatically as John narrates.)*

JOHN: The movement might have continued on this course for years if Michael had not received a letter that changed everything. It was from one of his victims. Michael had put him in the hospital for two weeks.

And when he got out, he was determined to track Michael down. But not for revenge. The beating had aroused feelings he had never before experienced. And he wanted more. He wanted Michael. In his letter, he professed his desire. And Michael was happy to oblige.

*(Jerry folds the letter and returns it to his pocket. As he concludes the presentation, he walks slowly forward to stand at John's side. Jerry's speech should end with both Jerry and John turning back toward Tim in disgust.)*

JERRY: That letter, and the breathless conversion that followed, prompted Michael to refocus his movement toward seduction rather than violence. He recruited women to join our ranks, and he renamed his movement "The Agenda." From that moment forward, we renounced violence. We began targeting the straight people most hostile to our kind by seducing them or their family members into the very lifestyle they publicly condemned. And when we had sucked enough into the fold, we planned to unleash the news of their newfound sexual proclivities to the world, making everyone see them for the vile hypocrites they were.

*(John and Jerry return to their places on either side of Tim, glowering at him.)*

PETER: *(Glib.)* And now the time has finally arrived. It's our coming out party! As we speak, reports are being sent to newspapers around the country, most with rather illuminating photos, about the homosexual adventures of more than fifty gay-bashing politicians, judges, and clergymen or their newly outed children, husbands, or wives. So no, Tim, you're not alone.

TIM: Wow. That was a really good answer. But, my God, Peter . . .

PETER: Yes, Tim, your god. That poor, distorted, manipulated, exploited deity. He's usually the one to blame, isn't he?

*(Peter begins to gather his things.)*

TIM: That's not what I meant . . .

PETER: And that's exactly my point. Nobody really means it when it comes to the big guy. Take care, Tim. We'll see you in tomorrow's paper. All of you.

*(Peter, John, and Jerry head for the door. Blackout.)*

END OF PLAY

# PLAYS FOR
# SIX OR MORE ACTORS

# Listeners

JANE MARTIN

*Listeners* was originally produced by Actors Theatre of Louisville at the 2006 Humana Festival. The cast was: Eleanor — Melinda Wade; Ralph — Mark Mineart; Walter — Jay Russell; Listeners — Tom Coiner; Lee Dolson; Ben Friesen; Aaron Alika Patinio. The director was Jon Jory.

CHARACTERS

ELEANOR

RALPH

WALTER

MAN 1

MAN 2

MAN 3

WOMAN 1

WOMAN 2

WOMAN 3

CHILD

SETTING

A home

. . .

*A home, represented by a single contemporary sofa and door frame.*
*Elsewhere, outside the "home" are three metal tables and chairs where men*
*in dark blue suits and red presidential ties sit with large earphones, listening*
*intently. In the blackout, we hear overlapping snatches of inane phone con-*
*versations. Lights up on Eleanor Leftwich, a neatly dressed woman in her*
*late thirties. She is on the phone.*

ELEANOR: And afterwards you fold in the beaten egg, one quarter cup of
chopped chives, a touch of Tabasco, bake at low heat and . . .
*(Two men also in dark blue suits and red ties appear at Eleanor's door. The*
*smaller, Walter, incongruously wears a porkpie hat. They knock.)*
Oh . . . uhmm, sorry, Mom. You just stay right there for two shakes of
a lamb's tail.
*(Opens door.)*
Hello.
RALPH: *(Naturally pronounced "Rafe.")* Hello.
ELEANOR: I —
RALPH: We —
ELEANOR: Are — ?
RALPH: Actually —
ELEANOR: Could — ?

RALPH: Absolutely —

WALTER: *(Bugs Bunny.)* What's up, Doc?

RALPH: Oh, let me guess. You are Eleanor Leftwich?

ELEANOR: I am.

RALPH: *(Delighted.)* Fantastic. I'm Rafe . . .

WALTER: Ralph.

RALPH: Rafe Aural, and allow me to say, Eleanor, I'm an admirer.

ELEANOR: An admirer?

RALPH: Your cries, murmurs and, might I say, exhortations during anal and oral sex are a treasured part of my day.

ELEANOR: I beg your pardon.

WALTER: *(Bogart.)* That's out of our hands, sweetheart.

RALPH: *(Gives Walter a little hit.)* Silly.

*(Brushes past Eleanor into the room.)*

Oh, this is lovely! Isn't this lovely, Walter? I could tell from your extensive vocabulary that you would have exquisite taste.

ELEANOR: But how . . .

WALTER: "But how . . . "

RALPH: Yes, we have our little ways.

*(Holding up phone.)*

Forgotten something?

ELEANOR: Oh, I'm on the phone.

RALPH: *(Holding it away from her.)* Well, if we know anything, we know that, don't we, Walter? Walter opines, by the way, that Tabasco really overpowers the recipe in an unhelpful way.

*(Speaks into phone.)*

Something's come up, dear, but she'll be back to you . . .

RALPH/WALTER: . . . In two shakes of a little lamb's tail.

*(Walter snaps cell phone shut.)*

ELEANOR: You cut off my call.

RALPH: I did, didn't I? That was naughty, wasn't it, Walter?

WALTER: Very naughty, Ralph.

RALPH: Rafe.

WALTER: Ralph.

ELEANOR: Excuse me, I haven't a clue who you are?

RALPH: *(To Walter.)* She hasn't a clue. Leftwich, you're a stitch. Honeybabydarlin'pet, you simply have to keep up here! All the little clicks, the little whirrs and . . .

RALPH/WALTER: *(Continued.)* faint beeps?

RALPH: The nice man the city sent to check your walls for killer mold?

WALTER: *(It was he.)* Ta-da!

RALPH: Land sakes alive, we're your Listeners, girl.

ELEANOR: Listeners?

RALPH: *(Shaking a warning finger.)* Oh, there are some saucy citizens simply slathering for a good listening to!

ELEANOR: I —

RALPH: Just teasing.

WALTER: *(John Wayne.)* Just teasing, citizen.

ELEANOR: I'm afraid you'll have to leave.

RALPH: Ah, I see . . . but really we mustn't, we can't, we've been assigned.

WALTER: Assigned!

RALPH: Assigned. Think of it this way, Eleanor Leftwich, consider us an instrument of increased intimacy.

RALPH/WALTER: It's a lonely life, *(Continued, for Ralph only.)* Eleanor.

RALPH: Who really, really listens to us? Who truly wants to hear us, know us, take us seriously,

RALPH/WALTER: hang on our words —

RALPH: — regard our emotionally chaotic and badly researched opinions as having heft, value, even profundity? Family, lovers, co-workers — they don't really hear us, do they? They are locked in the hell of self, Eleanor. Sadly, only your government cares.

ELEANOR: You heard me having sex?

RALPH: *(Reassuring.)* Really, it was almost as good as being there.

ELEANOR: But isn't that illegal?

*(Ralph and Walter laugh merrily.)*

RALPH: Time for the survey.

*(Walter flips open a folder and clears his throat.)*

Go it, Walter.

WALTER: Father, Shem Leftwich?

*(The survey section is done quick tempo.)*

ELEANOR: Slaughtered in Viet Nam on behalf of the domino theory.

WALTER: Uncle, Lowell Leftwich?

ELEANOR: Butchered in Panama, lest they should invade us.

WALTER: Auntie Crystal Leftwich, battlefield nurse?

ELEANOR: Cut down in Grenada insuring hegemony.

WALTER: Brother, Lefty Leftwich?

ELEANOR: Blown to smithereens, Desert Storm, guaranteeing full misogyny for all Kuwaitis.

WALTER: Brother Al?

RALPH: Lovely vocal register, brother Al.

WALTER: Lovely.

RALPH: Lovely.

ELEANOR: Friendly fire, Afghanistan.

WALTER: Brother Joe?

ELEANOR: Beheaded, castrated, dismembered in Iraq, insuring democracy and lollipops for all Islamic peoples.

RALPH: *(Thrilled.)* Good show, Eleanor, well done. Kudos for clarity. Haven't you just come through in the clutch?!

WALTER: Dabba dabba do.

RALPH: Sooooooo . . .

WALTER: Sooooooo . . .

RALPH: Our technologies have sensibly identified you, Eleanor, as a valued citizen who just might be a little cranky. And technologically speaking . . .

WALTER: You're a big fuckin' winner.

ELEANOR: I am?

RALPH: You are. Your mother, your friends, that sweet State Farm agent, whose untrammeled id has given Walter and me so much erotic pleasure, have elicited only idle interest, a little credit card browsing, the odd security check. But you, my intriguing Eleanor, if I may call you so, have hit the big time, a veritable coup, your own personal Listeners . . . us! Take our luggage to the guest room, Walter, down the hall, second left I believe.

ELEANOR: You hear everything I say here?

RALPH: We hear everything anyone says, Ms. Leftwich, anyone of the slightest interest.

ELEANOR: And someone hears you?

RALPH: Oh, Walter hears me, don't you, Walter?

WALTER: You wascally wabbit.

ELEANOR: And someone hears Walter?

RALPH: Agent Arthur in Bangor, Maine.

ELEANOR: And Arthur?

WALTER: Ziggy in New Rochelle.

ELEANOR: And Ziggy?

RALPH: Darlene in Cuttlefish, Kansas.

ELEANOR: And Darlene?

RALPH: Ryan in Tucumcari.

ELEANOR: And Ryan?

RALPH: Heard in Burbank.

WALTER: Who's heard in Baltimore.

RALPH: Who's heard in Bethesda.

WALTER: Who's heard at the C. I. of A.

RALPH: Who's heard in the war room.

RALPH/WALTER: Who's heard by . . .

RALPH: *(Stops. Speaks coyly.)* Oh, I don't know . . .

WALTER: He doesn't know.

RALPH: — heard perhaps by he who —

RALPH/WALTER: let us say —

RALPH: — hears all.

ELEANOR: *(Amazed.) He* listens?

RALPH: In the limitless soaring freedoms of democratic process, it is the bounden duty of he who serves only at our pleasure to attend to the fall of a sparrow or the infinitesimal vibration of the monarch's wing, dear Eleanor.

ELEANOR: *(Enthralled.)* So it's not inconceivable I could speak to him?

RALPH: Not inconceivable.

WALTER: The off-chance.

ELEANOR: So I'm not powerless? I could speak my heart, even here in the sanctuary of my home, and he who hears all might hear me?

RALPH: He might.

WALTER: He will.

RALPH: He cares.

> *(Eleanor looks up.)*

> Oh. Oh my. Do I espy upon your ivory cheek the silver tracery of a tear? Have you an unspoken sentiment, Eleanor?

ELEANOR: I can truly be heard? I never dreamed I could be heard?

RALPH: *(Shocked.)* Good heavens, Eleanor, you're not a tattooed tribeswoman of some dusky people's Banana Republic. You are the admired citizen of the most advanced society in the history of the world! Let freedom ring! Go to it, Walter.

WALTER: *(Putting on earphones that have been around his neck.)* 5, 4, 3, 2, 1 . . .

> *(Gives her the go signal.)*

ELEANOR: Now?

> *(Walter again signals "go.")*

> How should I address him?

WALTER: You swingin' dick.

RALPH: Walter! No honorifics necessary.

ELEANOR: *(Looking up.)* Sir? It's me, Citizen Leftwich.

*(A red light goes on at the desk of a Listener.)*

I mean, I'm nobody in particular, just a dental technician, sidelining in a little discreet hair removal, but I guess if . . . well, if you're really listening . . .

*(Another red light goes on.)*

I guess I'd really like to say . . .

*(Ralph gestures encouragingly.)*

Well, I'm kind of getting the feeling . . .

*(He gestures again.)*

. . . that you've fucked us all.

*(An alarm goes off in the distance. A curtain opens, and we see a man on a pedestal, suited as the others, in silhouette.)*

You've butchered our youth for dreams of empire, squandered our children's patrimony, enriched at untold social cost the inconceivably rich, battered our economy, ballooned our deficit, fractured our safety nets, demeaned the values that gave us pride in a national identity, fattened our cynicism . . .

*(A big red light.)*

. . . endangered our public education, made quislings of our librarians, dismantled our privacy, manipulated our fears, detained and tortured and bombed and killed men and women and children, appalled the world . . .

*(The silhouette figure drops his arm as a signal, and a red ring lights up on Ralph's hand.)*

. . . and all, all, all out of some blind, groping, self-serving, economic, geopolitical, theocratic impulse, untouched by real thought or empathy, at the behest of the entitled and corporate . . .

*(Ralph signals Walter, who moves behind her. Eleanor isn't focused on them. Ralph takes out and prepares a hypodermic.)*

. . . that can only end in the poisoning, beyond imagination, of our humanity and our poor Earth, you stupid, boorish, vulgar, avaricious, heartless, shallow, incomprehensible, smug, smarmy, illiterate prick!!

*(Walter grabs her from behind, covering her mouth. Ralph speaks admiringly while he administers the injection. She struggles but, by the end of Ralph's speech, goes limp.)*

RALPH: Well, by heaven, I'd have to say that's damned good listening! Shapely,

passionate, indelible rhetoric, nicely phrased in its indictments. I stamp that "superior" in anyone's blue book, Eleanor. Downright thrilling and absorbing and a by-God testament to why I got into the business.
*(Walter releases the body, and it crumples to the floor.)*
Good heavens, what a nasty fall.

WALTER: Kaput.

RALPH: No! You don't imagine a woman so vital and incisive with lovely breasts and a social conscience has taken her own life?

WALTER: Could be.

*(Scatters pills beside her and drops the bottle.)*

RALPH: Despair is a dangerous thing. But she wasn't boring. I enjoyed our repartee.

WALTER: Yeah, she had a mouth on her.

RALPH: Sometimes an assignment is just far too brief, Walter.

WALTER: Too brief.

*(Goes for the luggage.)*

RALPH: The problem is, of course, it all ends in paperwork.

*(A eulogy.)*
You are, or rather were, Eleanor Leftwich, living proof that a nation's purpose can only truly be defined by an articulate and loyal opposition.
*(Walter returns.)*
Her sun has set while it yet was day. Sleep, oh sleep, our daughter of the republic. A scrap of scripture, Walter.
*(They stand over her, heads bowed.)*

WALTER: *(Stentorian.)* "And I say, tell it not in Gath, nor publish it in the streets of Askelon."

RALPH: You said a mouthful there, Lord. Tempus fugit, Walter. Stitch in time saves nine.
*(They pick up the bags.)*
Set the moral compass, bosun.

WALTER: *(Woody Woodpecker laugh, followed by Porky Pig.)* That's all, folks.

RALPH: Never all, Walter, never all. Democracy without freedoms. Still only a work in progress.

WALTER: Getting closer though.

RALPH: Not beyond our reach.
*(They are out of the house and exiting.)*
Coming soon to an address near you.
*(Lights are dimming, shards and whispers of phone conversations rise.)*

WALTER: Well said, Ralph.

RALPH: Rafe.

WALTER: Ralph.

RALPH: Rafe. Up Donner, up Blitzen. Now fly away,

RALPH/WALTER: — fly away, fly away all!

(*They are gone. Only the body and the voices remain. Lights out.*)

WALTER: (*Woody Woodpecker laugh.*)


END OF PLAY


Note: Phone collage sound cue used at beginning and end of *Listeners*.

WOMAN: Grandma, it's Lilian, I just wanted to wish you . . .

MAN: . . . was the corporate secretary in charge organizing the board meetings and . . .

CHILD: I miss you, Daddy, will you bring me a . . .

2ND WOMAN: You think I care? I don't care. All that talk is just . . .

2ND MAN: . . . have no idea what the article means by "insurgent," so tell Jack . . .

WOMAN: . . . something called "left weave" jeans and I'm guessing the Gap, but I . . .

3RD MAN: Yeah, well if you could meet us in Aruba, I know Ellen would be pleased as . . .

CHILD: . . . but you'll miss my birthday, and I want . . .

2ND WOMAN: . . . a small bag of sand from the Bay of Pigs, but who's going to . . .

MAN: No, not Hamas, Hamas is . . .

3RD WOMAN: . . . completely volcanic . . .

WOMAN: So love and kisses, Grandma . . .

MAN: . . . as far as I know, but you know me and what I know, well, hell, what anybody knows . . . are you still there?

# Reading List

SUSAN MILLER

*Reading List* was produced in Vital Theatre Company's New Works Festival — December 15–18, 2005. It was directed by Cynthia Croot, with the following cast: Kathryn Grody, Maha Chehlaoui, Bridgit Antoinette Evans, Jay Smith, Michael Rudko, Happy Anderson.

CHARACTERS

*(Ages of the characters are just suggestions.)*

BERNIE: woman over forty. A librarian. Engaging. Modern. She loves her work. She could be anything, but she's this.

SNOW: man of indeterminate age. An astronomer. Experience and history show on him.

EAGAN: man in his forties. Filled with contemporary angst.

SONIA: woman in her thirties. A teacher. Urban.

MILO AND JACOB: played by the same actor, a man in his late twenties, early thirties. Milo is an FBI agent, earnest, but unsure. Jacob is a trucker, with good intentions.

JANEL: young woman, late teens. Original. Optimistic.

TIME

Present

SETTING

The suggestion of a Public Library

• • •

*Minimal setting to suggest a Public Library. Lush music (Sinatra's "One For My Baby") accompanies the Librarian, as she shreds pink sheets of paper. After a few moments, the music fades and she speaks directly to the audience.*

BERNIE: It used to be at the end of a day, I'd lock up and take myself out for a cocktail. Vodka straight up, three olives. I loved the olives. Well, and the word — cocktail.

*(Beat)*

My new ritual — I shred.

*(Beat)*

What it is, see, the powers of the Patriot Act give the government the right to review the records of people under suspicion of being suspicious. Which has been heinously interpreted to include the borrowing of books at libraries. So, I shred. Lists of things people want us to locate for them. A day's worth of requests. Like one I got yesterday asking where a woman might go if she needed shelter. And someone tracing the origin of a certain inflammatory phrase. Two queries regarding unpopular

Supreme Court rulings. And even the sacred hunt for some rapturous, quotidian, now too vulnerable detail.

*(Referring to a Pink Sheet)*

OK, here's someone asking for a volume on puppetry, which had a footnote containing an excerpt from "The Pink Code." Pink. Code. Words to alarm the vigilant homophobe. Actually, *Pink Code,* a book by a lovely man living in Maine, I've since learned — we're in correspondence — is a manual for the use of color and hue in animation. Who knew? Puppets are apparently staging a comeback.

*(She shreds it. Then:)*

It keeps me going. What people have on their minds.

*(A hesitant man walks up to her desk.)*

JACOB: Hello.

BERNIE: *(Taken with his shy formality)* Hello.

JACOB: I was wondering . . . there are so many . . . you know, well, books . . . in here. I was thinking if you could maybe narrow it down for me, recommend one. Your personal pick.

BERNIE: *(Continued.)* *(To audience.)* This fellow, he glowed. As if it were his first time in a library. Excited by information but embarrassed by it, too.

JACOB: Something to keep me in place. Something I could — come back to. See, I'm on the road. I'm miles from anything. Whatever you got.

BERNIE: *(To audience)* It thrilled me. I mean, a long haul truck driver, taking the time, wanting to know. Who punishes curiosity? But then, I project a scenario. They'd go to his house — this is what I imagined — they'd go to his house, the FBI or whoever they send. They'd already know he pays his taxes. I mean, they'd probably know a fair amount about him, right? Then they look into things and his wife has a Middle Eastern name. He drives a truck. He could be carrying materials. See where this goes. He's obviously a threat, this man who glows in the library and drives to the point of collapse to reach his destination. A man who's gotten himself some books so he doesn't get into trouble on route. He stops for the night. Coffee.

JACOB: No hookers.

BERNIE *(Continued.)* And he reads. So he can answer his kids' school questions.

JACOB: And stay honest regarding my vows.

*(Bernie hands him a book.)*

BERNIE: He reads to keep the stark, abstract fatigue from bearing loneliness. He doesn't want another sexually transmitted disease, either. He's taken out three hard cover volumes. He likes the look of them. The heft. The pages against his rough hands. He's working over a passage in Steinbeck. It just sneaks up on him.

JACOB: *(Looking at pages in awe.)* I didn't know. How it could — I just didn't know this. I didn't know a person could think of this.

BERNIE: So, what could there be about a man crying under a moonlit sky in the cab of his Freightliner Classic XL that sends out a warning to the government?

*(A man, Eagan, seated at a table, looks up from his book and speaks, his rapid delivery makes his ruminations almost comic, were it not for real turmoil:)*

EAGAN: The stars. I was looking up anything I could find on the stars. There was this article about dark matter that scared the shit out of me, and I was putting my whole family through hell about it. Just the way my daughter has pushed me to my limits with her inquiries into the absurdity of language and meaning. Meaning there is none. No meaning. Which I take as bleak and troublesome coming like that from a young person. And, I guess, it challenged something deep and confronted me on a personal level. Like my fatherhood, my being a parent was all of a sudden a pointless and sorry thing. I like talking at the dinner table. It's time well spent if you put aside other concerns. But, I was depressing everyone, and I thought maybe there's another way, you know, with more information, to look at things. To look at this dark matter and my daughter's questions and turn it all into a metaphor of well-being instead of what it clearly represented to me now as a crushing void with the power to cancel the present, past, and future. Life, albeit the sad and confusing thing though it is, still, it is what we know. And what we want our children to know. Well, apparently in my investigations of the universe there were more than a couple of references to a certain gay astronomer. He kept turning up in the materials I happened to look through. And they wanted to know — they being the messengers of secrecy and harbingers of silence — what I had to do with him. What interest did I have in a gay astronomer who was fired from his post in the fifties, and what business did I have with footnotes that referred to the incident in the park, and did I know him.

*(Beat)*

Well, no, but I want to fucking know him now.

*(The Astronomer, Snow, comes out from the stacks.)*

SNOW: So, what do you want to know?

EAGAN: What happened?

SNOW: What happened was what happens.

*(Beat)*

I was reading maps with the U.S. Army Map Service. Something I loved doing. Ever since I was a boy. The whole idea of — I don't know, pinpointing a place you can find again and again. Well, this one night — it was late. I was on my way home, and I stopped for awhile to see the moonlight in Lafayette Park across from the White House. The light fell on two men. Kissing. And I was thinking how beautiful they were. How just — well, that. When the cops descended.

EAGAN: And what? They arrested you for just being there?

SNOW: You're in the vicinity, you must be gay. You're gay — you're implicated. I was taken in for investigation of a morals charge. It was dropped, but I was fired from my job. And — I don't know how to say this without coming off as some kind of fallen protagonist in post-war B-movie America — I was banned from all future employment with the federal government.

EAGAN: But you have a Ph.D. from Goddam Harvard. You were a World War Two combat veteran, for Chrissakes.

SNOW: Yeah. And I was a Jewish queer in a blue state.

EAGAN: Well, there are plenty of other things to be afraid of. Like, for fucking example, the void in the universe.

SNOW: Not as terrifying as gays having their kiss or marrying, though.

EAGAN: Your name in a footnote putting people in my business is what scares me. Well, and our finite time on the planet.

SNOW: I have a bad feeling everyone's going to know more than they want to about what it's like to get comfortable with hiding. Living in code. It makes for an anxious world.

EAGAN: Just — I don't get how people with no virtue other than they're straight or white or claim God's on their side, have the power to ruin lives.

SNOW: And the crazy thing is, if our ideas, our acts could be seen, we'd be able to see ourselves. And wouldn't it be better to be judged in full view? Because we all bear scrutiny.

EAGAN: I think my daughter is gay. I want to tell her something. About you. About the Earth from a distance.

SNOW: We're grand and possible from a distance. But, we live here.

*(Lights on another area. Milo, an FBI agent, approaches Sonia's door.)*

MILO: Sonia Federman?

SONIA: Yes?

MILO: Are you in possession of library books, the titles of which are —

SONIA: *(Overlapping.)* They send people now? They send actual people to come to your house and collect fines? God, I know they're overdue. I was meaning to bring them back ages ago. Well, anyhow, what do I owe?

MILO: *(Showing his badge,)* Can you tell me where your parents were born?

SONIA: What?

MILO: What country are your parents from?

SONIA: Do they have books overdue?

MILO: *(Thrown by her.)* I really don't know. Federman — it sounds foreign.

SONIA: We're pretty much all foreign, aren't we?

MILO: Meaning?

SONIA: We all come from somewhere else. If you trace it back. You know, give me your tired and your poor, your huddled masses yearning to breathe free.

MILO: Huddled masses.

*(Beat)*

Lenin?

SONIA: Emma Lazarus. Statue of Liberty.

MILO: *(Embarrassed not to have known.)* Right. Right. So, just to verify. You're a teacher in the public school system?

SONIA: Senior English and drama. I taught ninth grade for a while but they were all about turning into the next thing not the thing they were, and it was pretty much totally bogus totally all of the time.

MILO: Drama. That's putting on plays. You put on plays?

SONIA: We read plays.

MILO: You don't put them on? I thought you had to put plays on.

SONIA: Well, you can put them on. Some people put them on. But this is a literature class. We read them.

MILO: And these plays, you took them out of the public library.

SONIA: They didn't have them in the school library.

MILO: So, the school didn't authorize them.

SONIA: They didn't not authorize them. I do this all the time. We all do. Supplementary materials. Oil for education, not so much left for books. We all do this.

MILO: *(Reading titles on his notepad.)* There's *A Dead Mule in the Street. Silverstein & Company. It's Our Town, Too. My Burka, Your Bris.* Do these play titles sound familiar to you?

SONIA: You want them back. I'll get them. Jesus.

MILO: I tried out for one in school. A play. I mainly wanted to get next to a girl named Cheryl. I wanted to touch her sweater. She was in all the plays. She was in the halls. She was everywhere. I wanted to get her pregnant.

SONIA: You wanted to get her pregnant?

MILO: In the play. The guy in the play.

SONIA: Your character.

MILO: My character. He wanted to. I would've — I mean, me myself, who I am, I would've pulled out.

SONIA: Do you remember what play this was?

MILO: I kissed her. And I said something. I don't know if it was even in the play the words I used. And then I got an erection and I didn't get the part, and Cheryl, she sees it. She sees I'm hard and says to the drama coach I think he'd be good in the part.

SONIA: Maybe he didn't want her to get pregnant. You know? It was the dramatic event. It was messy. It complicated things. That's why it was in the play, probably. I mean, you would have been careful. But then your life isn't literature.

MILO: I have to do this, you know. I'm in the world of undercover. I'm looking for inconsistencies and subtexts. Subtexts of peril. I don't just wait for it to unravel. I'm supposed to recognize a warning.

SONIA: We're the same then. Always looking for something. Except, I don't report people for their thoughts. Or their questions. Or their boners.

MILO: I'm sorry I let that slip. I didn't mean anything toward you. I'm not —

SONIA: I know the moment of taking someone else's words, of thinking them, of being in a play and interpreting someone else's idea of things. Because we can. We can kiss and not actually get pregnant. We can subvert ideas and reconstruct history and express ourselves with our cocks and our breasts and our intellect and our hands all over each other. We can say what we mean and don't mean and might do and would never do and get hard and wet and thankful. That's why I took those plays out of the library. That's what you can do in a play.

MILO: I have to make a report. I have to write something down. I have to say something.

SONIA: "It is difficult to get the news from poems but men die miserably every day for lack of what is found there." Say that.

*(Lights up on Bernie.)*

BERNIE: *(To audience.)* When I was a girl, I wanted to be a choreographer. I didn't know what a choreographer was. It just sounded good. So, my father sent me to the dictionary. Go look it up, he said. Go to the library and look it up. And I looked up as many words as I could so I could stay there all afternoon. I went to the shelves and opened books to passages that were exciting even though I didn't understand most of what I read. There was always something I found wherever the books fell open that kept me coming back. And keeps me. To this day.

*(Janel approaches the desk and hands Bernie a piece of paper.)*

JANEL: I know I shouldn't be asking, Miss Bernie, but I was sleepless over that novel you got me started on, and I have a paper due on something not anywhere near as compelling, so if you could just find this one fact I need, or tell me where I could, you'd be my hero.

BERNIE: Did you try the Internet?

JANEL: That's just a thing that leads me astray. And it doesn't have the same good smell as in here. Whiff of pencils and eraser. The dusty stirring paper thing.

BERNIE: *(Pleased, enjoying her.)* So, did you get to that passage where I put the Post-it?

JANEL: It was wicked original. And sad, a little bit.

BERNIE: I've got something else I want to show you — but not until after you turn in your paper. Deal?

JANEL: I can't totally make that promise.

*(Bernie takes the paper from Janel and walks to stacks.)*

JANEL: *(Continued.)* *(To audience.)* My librarian. She's always got a list of things for me to read. I do that thing with people. Make them mine. Anyhow, sometimes she just sends me to the stacks and says, just take any book. Read the first sentence. Tells me, "Janel, one thing leads to another. You go to a place you didn't think was where you needed to go, and it maybe takes you to the place you were meant to find."

*(Eagan, sitting nearby, responds to her.)*

EAGAN: But what if on our way to the thing we were meant to find, we come across a — paragraph, a footnote, something irreverent, something ardent and unpopular. Does that make you part of a conspiracy? Or are you just part of the fabric of things, part of the mystery, searching for some place to land.

*(Bernie re-enters.)*

BERNIE: *(To audience.)* An older person came up to me very distressed one day. She said, "There is a giant — well — organ," she said. "On the screen and I can't get it off." New way to flash someone, I guess. Well, no, we don't want to encourage people in the library to surf pornography on the Internet. We don't want that. But what becomes of us when a place that gives permission to get lost in a book is turned into a place where you can be found. What do you call that?

*(Then echoing her father.)*

Go. Look it up!

*(Milo walks in.)*

MILO: Excuse me, I need a poem.

BERNIE: You need a poem.

MILO: I'm looking for a poem. Can you get me a poem?

BERNIE: Which one?

MILO: I don't know.

BERNIE: Well, can you give me a line or something to go on. The name of the poet.

MILO: A poem about a poem.

BERNIE: You'd think that would narrow the field.

MILO: How about a play, then?

BERNIE: We've got plays. Again, though —

MILO: A great play.

BERNIE: About heroes or love or one person's place in the sweep of history or betrayal, redemption, loss?

*(He refers to his notebook.)*

MILO: The one about a Streetcar. Or a Salesman. Or a Town. Or, Angels. Or — a Raisin? Do you have any of those?

BERNIE: *(Surprisingly moved by him.)* We have them all. Every one.

*(She walks toward stacks, speaking to audience.)*

You know, some librarians go to jail for this. For giving someone a play. A poem. Losing sleep and teeth and years in prison. This is hard for us here to know. We don't see what goes on in other places. This is how we're imprisoned in this country. By not seeing.

*(Bernie offers some books to Milo.)*

JANEL: *(To the entire place.)* Listen up! I want to make a bitch beautiful poem to my librarians in other places.

*(A moment. Then, in spoken word, def poetry jam style:)*

Someone gives you a book

Don't close it

She chose it

Turn a page to possess it

Finesse it

Stress on the words that repeat you

Any life can complete you
Arranged on a shelf is a wealth is your stealth
Is the health of your mind and my mind is my own and I own
what I know, what I don't, what I will when I chill with the
pages I read when I need to know
So, my eyes are wide to go inside and find what's behind the
world unfurled when I open a book
Yo, open a book. Don't hurl it.
*(After a moment, one by one, everyone in the library begins reading out loud
from his or her books. This builds, until their lush cacophony fills the air.)*
*(Bernie takes in the music of words. Then, as if issuing a sweeping challenge
to anyone who would silence this joyful noise:)*
BERNIE: Shred that!

END OF PLAY

# The *Mary Celeste*

## Don Nigro

The *Mary Celeste* was first produced on February 10, 2006 by the Drove Theatre Company at the Greenwich Street Theatre in New York City with the following cast: Sophia Matilda — Kate Kenney; Sarah — Danielle Liccardo; Captain — Doug Durlacher; First Voice — Reyna de Courcy; Second Voice — Rebecca Servon; Third Voice — William Schmincke. Directed by Kevin Kittle and Zetna Fuentes. Costume design by David Withrow. Produced by Reyna de Courcy and Kate Kenney of the Gravity & Glass Theatre Company.

CHARACTERS

    SOPHIA MATILDA: a young woman
    SARAH: her mother
    CAPTAIN: her father
    FIRST VOICE: a girl
    SECOND VOICE: a woman
    THIRD VOICE: a man

SETTING

A few wooden chairs and a table surrounded by darkness.

THE VOICES

The voices are onstage but not visible, hidden in the darkness that surrounds the three characters we can see. They should always be done live and onstage in the dark. They should not be recorded.

This whispering in the shadows begins when the play begins and ends when the play ends. It never stops during the play, but at the beginning it is so quiet that the audience should hardly be aware of it. It will become louder as indicated in the course of the text, but at no time should it become so loud that we can't understand what the three characters we can see are saying.

The First Voice whispers a continuous looped monologue made up entirely of Sophia Matilda's lines in order from beginning to end, with the responses of the other characters omitted and with no breaks at all. When the First Voice comes to the end of these lines, she simply starts up again at the beginning and moves through them again, as many times as is necessary until the play ends.

The Second Voice whispers a continuous looped monologue made up entirely of Sarah's lines in order from beginning to end, with the responses of the other characters omitted and with no breaks at all. As with the First Voice, she is on a loop, so when she comes to the last of the lines she simply starts at the beginning again, with no break.

The Third Voice whispers a continuous looped monologue made up entirely of the Captain's lines in order from beginning to end, with the responses of the other characters omitted and with no breaks at all. As with the First and Second Voices, he is on a loop, so when he comes to the last of the lines he simply starts at the beginning again, with no break.

The Voices are always speaking, all three at the same time. They never take turns. They go on, regardless of what each other or the actors we can see are saying. Often a happy convergence will cause a brief pause in the dialogue of the three visible characters to coincide with something spoken by the voices that seems very appropriate to the moment. When it does, this is good, but don't expect it to happen that way every night. Just keep going and trust the serendipity of events to take care of what will be audible behind the dialogue in each performance. It's not necessary for it to ever come out exactly the same twice.

For the convenience of the performers, the monologues of the Voices are printed at the end of the text.

• • •

*Sound of the ocean, wind, gulls, the gentle creaking of a ship. Lights up on Sophia Matilda, a young woman. We see her as she is in the year 1900. Her parents are as she remembers them, or imagines them, on the ship* Mary Celeste, *in November of the year 1872. In the background, so faint at first that we can barely hear them, the Voices are whispering together.*

SOPHIA MATILDA: Sailed for Genoa, fifth of November. A month later, the ship found drifting off the coast of Portugal. Nobody on deck. Nobody below. The beds unmade, the bedding damp. But everything in its place. A spool of thread. Music open on the harmonium. A half-eaten meal on the table, some said. An open bottle of medicine. The clock stopped.
*(Brief pause. Voices just a bit more audible. Then the sound of a ticking clock.)*
My mother used to tell me stories.

SARAH: Once upon a time there was a little girl who sailed across the water.

CAPTAIN: Why don't you make the beds?

SARAH: I'll make the beds.

SOPHIA MATILDA: The seamen's chests were all in place and dry, their oilskin boots and pipes. The last date in the log book showed the *Mary Celeste* passed Santa Maria Island at eight in the morning on November 25th. The ship was found five hundred miles away, on course. The Captain, his wife, their little girl, and the crew had vanished.
*(Sounds of creaking and groaning.)*

SARAH: A person could go mad with all the thumping and bumping, the shaking and tossing back and forth of the cargo, and such odd screechings and growlings from the hold that seem to get worse the further we get from land. What kind of ship is this, to make such noises?

CAPTAIN: Grain alcohol in a red oak cask will sweat and groan in the heat. Get hundreds of them together in one enclosed space and you have a chorus of demons.

SARAH: I don't think I like this ship.

CAPTAIN: There's nothing wrong with the ship. It's a good enough ship.

SARAH: The cook says it's an unlucky ship.

CAPTAIN: The cook's a wet-nosed imbecile.

SARAH: He's not. He's a very nice boy. He says it's always been an unlucky ship.

CAPTAIN: What does the cook know about my ship? He's barely old enough to shave.

SARAH: The older sailors told him. They all know. The first captain died two days after she was registered. On the maiden voyage she wrecked on the coast of Maine. She caught fire once. And then she collided with another ship and sank it in the Straits of Dover. Then she ran aground on Cape Breton Island. She's been sold and sold again. And worst of all, the name was changed.

CAPTAIN: What the devil has the name got to do with anything?

SARAH: It's terrible luck to change the name of a ship, the sailors say. And there was dry rot in the timbers.

CAPTAIN: She's got a copper lining now. That isn't going to rot.

SOPHIA MATILDA: They found brown stains on the deck that might have been blood, and stains the same color on an old Italian sword found under the Captain's bunk.

SARAH: They think the ship is haunted.

CAPTAIN: Why is my wife spending all her time talking to sailors when there are beds to be made? Why do you talk to sailors at all? Sailors are worse than a boatload of superstitious, gossiping old women.

SARAH: Well, I've got to talk to somebody.

CAPTAIN: Talk to me.

SARAH: You're too busy to talk to me.

CAPTAIN: I'm the Captain. I've things to do. Talk to your child, if you want to talk.

SARAH: My child is a child. I am not.

SOPHIA MATILDA: The Court of Enquiry couldn't decide what happened, so they just had the cargo delivered, and the ship sold again, then run aground on purpose for the insurance money. But that captain died, another went mad, and another hung himself, I heard. But some of that might not be true.

*(The whispering of the Voices has gotten just a bit louder.)*

SARAH: And I've been having the strangest dreams since I came on board. One night I dreamed the ship was full of ticking clocks.

CAPTAIN: Nobody cares about your dreams.

SARAH: Another night I dreamed a giant squid attacked the ship, reaching its tentacles in the portholes to pluck us out, one by one, and stuffing us into its mouth.

CAPTAIN: Don't say things like that around the child. Do you want to frighten her to death? What's the matter with you?

SARAH: I don't know. I've been feeling quite strange lately. Imagining things just around corners. Lying awake at night and listening to those horrible creakings and groanings from the hold. And it isn't just me. Volkert and Boz said they saw something creeping up the steps.

CAPTAIN: Volkert and Boz have hardly a brain between them.

SARAH: And Albert's been in despair.

CAPTAIN: He misses his wife. He'll get over it.

SARAH: Even Sophia Matilda has been seeing things.

CAPTAIN: Our child has not been seeing things. The foolishness she hears you talking gets into her head.

SARAH: She says she hears voices whispering in the night.

*(The Voices are louder now. We can perhaps just begin to make out a stray word or two now and then.)*

CAPTAIN: The child is daft. Just like her mother.

SOPHIA MATILDA: It was cold when we left, but it grew warmer as we got farther and farther from land, and the warmer it got, the more I could hear the voices whispering in the darkness.

CAPTAIN: She's talking gibberish. She's a little child.

SARAH: Edward said that children can often sense things before others do.

CAPTAIN: Edward? Who's Edward?

SARAH: The cook.

CAPTAIN: You call him Edward?

SARAH: That's his name.

CAPTAIN: Oh. That's his name, is it? And what does he call you?

SARAH: Just what is that supposed to mean?

SOPHIA MATILDA: Here is the question we don't wish to ask: How can we know what happens when we're not there? How can we know what happens when somebody else is there, but not us? How can we trust what others tell us? Or, how can we know what happens in the past? Or if perhaps one was there, in the past, but was a very small child, who thinks she remembers something, but can't be sure. How can we tell memory from imagination or desire? How can we trust what we think we remember? I think I remember a ship full of voices whispering in the dark.

SARAH: Edward. Edward. Edward. I can say his name if I like.

CAPTAIN: It isn't a healthy thing for the Captain's wife to be spending so much time cooped up in close quarters with the cook.

SARAH: Well, where do you suggest I go? Should I take a stroll in the ocean? Would you like that?

SOPHIA MATILDA: This story will be told a thousand times, and people will offer a thousand explanations, and some of them will seem to make more sense than others, some will be written by honest people trying to understand and some by people trying to profit from our tragedy and some will be written by very sincere lunatics, but none of these explanations has the power to satisfy, since all explanations are lies, just as all pleasure is anticlimax.

CAPTAIN: What have you been doing with the cook?

SARAH: What have I been doing with the cook?

CAPTAIN: What have you been doing with the cook?

SARAH: Cooking. I've been cooking with the cook.

CAPTAIN: And what have you been cooking?

SARAH: You know what we've been cooking. You've been eating it.

CAPTAIN: What have I been eating?

SARAH: You don't know what you've been eating?

CAPTAIN: The food's been tasting funny all this voyage. Have you been poisoning me?

SARAH: No, but there's a thought. Do we have any rat poison left?

CAPTAIN: Maybe we should ask the cook.

SARAH: Maybe we should ask everybody on the ship. Maybe we should ask whoever's been whispering in our daughter's ears.

CAPTAIN: Keep your voice down. The child will hear.

SARAH: Since when have you been concerned about my child?

CAPTAIN: She's my child, too, isn't she?

SARAH: It pleases you to think so.

CAPTAIN: What are you saying? What are you saying to me?

(*The Voices are louder now.*)

SARAH: I'm not saying anything to you. You must be hearing the voices whispering. Sometimes you look as if you did. You look as if you're listening to something. The sailors say before a person drowns, they hear the mermaids whispering. Edward says —

CAPTAIN: Shut up. Shut up. Shut up.

SARAH: Don't tell me to shut up.

CAPTAIN: I don't mean you. I mean the voices.

SARAH: So you hear them, too?

CAPTAIN: It must be the casks. The alcohol in the heat.

SARAH: Or maybe you've been sneaking down there and drinking it.

CAPTAIN: You can't drink that. It's poison. It will drive you mad.

SARAH: At this point, madness might be a relief.

CAPTAIN: I've heard of crews driven mad by fumes from the cargo.

SARAH: Did you hear that? Be quiet a minute and listen.

    *(The Voices are louder.)*

CAPTAIN: I've heard of ships exploding on the sea.

SARAH: Listen. I can almost make out what they're saying.

CAPTAIN: We've got to get off this ship.

SARAH: Wait. I want to listen.

CAPTAIN: Sarah. We've got to get off this ship. Get the child.

SARAH: I don't want to leave. They're trying to tell me something. Edward
    says —

CAPTAIN: Get the child. Now. Get her now. Now.

SARAH: They're trying to tell us that —

CAPTAIN: Now. Get her now.

    *(Sound of the Voices and of horrible creaking and groaning from the hold.)*

SOPHIA MATILDA: In my dream the whispering and groaning and screaming
    are all mixed together. There's panic everywhere. I'm being clutched by
    my mother, handed off to a sailor, put into a boat. The voices are whis-
    pering and shrieking. Someone cuts away the boat with an ax. No time
    to do anything properly. Down into the water.

    *(The Voices begin to grow quieter, gradually.)*

    In my dream, the ship is receding from us. We can't get back to it. It gets
    smaller and smaller, and we're left alone on the ocean, and the voices
    fade away, the voices fade. And then it gets dark, all huddled together,
    and the ocean swallows us.

SARAH: Once upon a time there was a little girl who sailed across the water.

    *(The Voices very quiet now, faint whispering.)*

SOPHIA MATILDA: They say I was found on the shore. I'd been lashed to some-
    thing. The people who found me never reported it because they were
    afraid someone would come to take me away. They could have no chil-
    dren of their own. They loved me and took care of me. Later, a raft with
    seven dead men washed up on shore. It might have been the crew.

Nobody could tell for sure. What happened to my mother and my father, nobody could say.

*(The Voices begin to get louder again.)*

But more and more now, I am hearing the voices again. I am hearing the voices in my head at night. At night I go out and look at the ocean. What the ocean spares, it takes again, in time. When there's no moon, and a bit of fog, you can't tell where the sky ends and the ocean begins. But you can hear them in the water, in the darkness, if you listen.

*(Sound of the Voices growing louder and louder as the light fades on her. When the light goes out, the voices fade, and all we can hear are the sound of the ticking clock and the ocean and gull sounds. Then the clock stops.)*

### END OF PLAY

•   •   •

### APPENDIX: THE THREE VOICES

FIRST VOICE: Sailed for Genoa, fifth of November. A month later, the ship found drifting off the coast of Portugal. Nobody on deck. Nobody below. The beds unmade, the bedding damp. But everything in its place. A spool of thread. Music open on the harmonium. A half-eaten meal on the table, some said. An open bottle of medicine. The clock stopped. My mother used to tell me stories. The seamen's chests were all in place and dry, their oilskin boots and pipes. The last date in the log book showed the *Mary Celeste* passed Santa Maria Island at eight in the morning on November 25th. The ship was found five hundred miles away, on course. The Captain, his wife, their little girl, and the crew had vanished. They found brown stains on the deck that might have been blood, and stains the same color on an old Italian sword found under the Captain's bunk. The Court of Enquiry couldn't decide what happened, so they just had the cargo delivered, and the ship sold again, then run aground on purpose for the insurance money. But that captain died, another went mad, and another hung himself, I heard. But some of that might not be true. It was cold when we left, but it grew warmer as we got farther and farther from land, and the warmer it got, the more I could hear the voices whispering in the darkness. Here is the question we don't wish to ask: How can we know what happens when we're not there? How can we know what happens when somebody else is there, but not us? How can we trust what others tell us? Or, how can we know what happens in the past? Or if perhaps one was there, in the past, but was a very small child, who thinks she remembers something, but can't be sure. How can we tell memory from imagination or desire? How can we trust what we think we remember? I think I remember a ship full of voices whispering in the dark. This story will be told a thousand times, and people will offer a thousand explanations, and some of them will seem to make more sense than others, some will be written by honest people trying to understand and some by people trying to profit from our tragedy and some will be written by very sincere lunatics, but none of these explanations has the power to satisfy, since all explanations are lies, just as all pleasure is anti-climax. In my dream the whispering and groaning and screaming are all mixed together. There's panic everywhere. I'm being clutched by my mother, handed off to a sailor, put into a boat. The voices are whisper-ing and shrieking. Someone cuts away the boat with an ax. No time to do anything properly. Down into the water. In my dream, the ship is receding from us. We can't get back to it. It gets smaller and smaller, and we're left alone on the ocean, and the voices fade away, the voices fade. And then it gets dark, all huddled together, and the ocean swallows us. They say I was found on the shore. I'd been lashed to something. The people who found me never reported it because they were afraid some-one would come to take me away. They could have no children of their own. They loved me and took care of me. Later, a raft with seven dead men washed up on shore. It might have been the crew. Nobody could tell for sure. What happened to my mother and my father, nobody could say. But more and more now, I am hearing the voices again. I am hear-ing the voices in my head at night. At night I go out and look at the ocean. What the ocean spares, it takes again, in time. When there's no moon, and a bit of fog, you can't tell where the sky ends and the ocean begins. But you can hear them in the water, in the darkness, if you listen.

SECOND VOICE: Once upon a time there was a little girl who sailed across the water. I'll make the beds. A person could go mad with all the thumping and bumping, the shaking and tossing back and forth of the cargo, and such odd screechings and growlings from the hold that seem to get worse the further we get from land. What kind of ship is this, to make such noises? I don't think I like this ship. The cook says it's an unlucky ship. He's not. He's a very nice boy. He says it's always been an unlucky ship.

The older sailors told him. They all know. The first captain died two days after she was registered. On the maiden voyage she wrecked on the coast of Maine. She caught fire once. And then she collided with another ship and sank it in the Straits of Dover. Then she ran aground on Cape Breton Island. She's been sold and sold again. And worst of all, the name was changed. It's terrible luck to change the name of a ship, the sailors say. And there was dry rot in the timbers. They think the ship is haunted. Well, I've got to talk to somebody. You're too busy to talk to me. My child is a child. I am not. And I've been having the strangest dreams since I came on board. One night I dreamed the ship was full of ticking clocks. Another night I dreamed a giant squid attacked the ship, reaching its tentacles in the portholes to pluck us out, one by one, and stuffing us into its mouth. I don't know. I've been feeling quite strange lately. Imagining things just around corners. Lying awake at night and listening to those horrible creakings and groanings from the hold. And it isn't just me. Volkert and Boz said they saw something creeping up the steps. And Albert's been in despair. Even Sophia Matilda has been seeing things. She says she hears voices whispering in the night. Edward said that children can often sense things before others do. The cook. That's his name. Just what is that supposed to mean? Edward. Edward. Edward. I can say his name if I like. Well, where do you suggest I go? Should I take a stroll in the ocean? Would you like that? What have I been doing with the cook? Cooking. I've been cooking with the cook. You know what we've been cooking. You've been eating it. You don't know what you've been eating? No, but there's a thought. Do we have any rat poison left? Maybe we should ask everybody on the ship. Maybe we should ask whoever's been whispering in our daughter's ears. Since when have you been concerned about my child? It pleases you to think so. I'm not saying anything to you. You must be hearing the voices whispering. Sometimes you look as if you did. You look as if you're listening to something. The sailors say before a person drowns, they hear the mermaids whispering. Edward says — Don't tell me to shut up. So you hear them, too? Or maybe you've been sneaking down there and drinking it. At this point, madness might be a relief. Did you hear that? Be quiet a minute and listen. Listen. I can almost make out what they're saying. Wait. I want to listen. I don't want to leave. They're trying to tell me something. Edward says — They're trying to tell us that — Once upon a time there was a little girl who sailed across the water.

THIRD VOICE: Why don't you make the beds? Grain alcohol in a red oak cask will sweat and groan in the heat. Get hundreds of them together in one enclosed space and you have a chorus of demons. There's nothing wrong with the ship. It's a good enough ship. The cook's a wet-nosed imbecile. What does the cook know about my ship? He's barely old enough to shave. What the devil has the name got to do with anything? She's got a copper lining now. That isn't going to rot. Why is my wife spending all her time talking to sailors when there are beds to be made? Why do you talk to sailors at all? Sailors are worse than a boatload of superstitious, gossiping old women. Talk to me. I'm the Captain. I've things to do. Talk to your child, if you want to talk. Nobody cares about your dreams. Don't say things like that around the child. Do you want to frighten her to death? What's the matter with you? Volkert and Boz have hardly a brain between them. He misses his wife. He'll get over it. Our child has not been seeing things. The foolishness she hears you talking gets into her head. The child is daft. Just like her mother. She's talking gibberish. She's a little child. Edward? Who's Edward? You call him Edward? Oh. That's his name, is it? And what does he call you? It isn't a healthy thing for the Captain's wife to be spending so much time cooped up in close quarters with the cook. What have you been doing with the cook? What have you been doing with the cook? And what have you been cooking? What have I been eating? The food's been tasting funny all this voyage. Have you been poisoning me? Maybe we should ask the cook. Keep your voice down. The child will hear. She's my child, too, isn't she? What are you saying? What are you saying to me? Shut up. Shut up. Shut up. I don't mean you. I mean the voices. It must be the casks. The alcohol in the heat. You can't drink that. It's poison. It will drive you mad. I've heard of crews driven mad by fumes from the cargo. I've heard of ships exploding on the sea. We've got to get off this ship. Sarah. We've got to get off this ship. Get the child. Get the child. Now. Get her now. Now. Now. Get her now.

# Permission Acknowledgments

*The Agenda.* © 2007 by Paul Siefken. Reprinted by permission of the author. For performance rights, contact the author c/o The Drilling Co., 107 W. 82nd St. #1A, New York, N.Y. 10024.

*Body Shop.* © 2007 by Anne Phelan. Reprinted by permission of the author. For performance rights, contact Smith and Kraus, Inc. (www.smithandkraus.com) E-mail: sandk@sover.net

*Bruce.* © 2007 by C. Denby Swanson. Reprinted by permission of the author. For performance rights, contact Maura Teitelbaum, Abrams Artists, 275 7th Ave., New York, N.Y. 10001.

*Cardinal Rule.* © 2007 by Emily DeVoti. Reprinted by permission of Jonathan Lomma, William Morris Agency, Inc., 1325 Avenue of the Americas, New York, N.Y. 10019.

*Come Into the Garden, Maud.* © 2007 by Don Nigro. Reprinted by permission of the author. For performance rights, contact the author: jnigro@neo.rr.com

*The Concorde Fallacy.* © 2005 by Doug Rand. Reprinted by permission of Playscripts, Inc., which publishes the play separately in an acting edition, and which handles performance rights. Contact information: www.playscripts.com (Web site), info@playscripts.com (e-mail), 866-NEW-PLAY (telephone).

*The Deal.* © 2005 by Kate McCamey. Reprinted by permission of the author. For performance rights, contact the author (katemccamey@yahoo.com).

*Dining Outdoors.* © 2007 by Vincent Delaney. Reprinted by permission of the author. For performance rights, contact Smith and Kraus, Inc. (www.smithandkraus.com) E-mail: sandk@sover.net

*Dog Lovers.* © 2007 by S. W. Senek. Reprinted by permission of the author. For performance rights, contact Original Works Online Publishing, 4611-1/2 Ambrose Ave, Los Angeles, CA 90027. Web site: www.originalworksonline.com

*Epiphany.* © 2007 by Frederick Stroppel. Reprinted by permission of the author. For performance rights, contact the author (fredstrop@aol.com).

*Fog.* © 2007 by Don Nigro. Reprinted by permission of the author. For performance rights, contact the author: jnigro@neo.rr.com

*Grave.* © 2005 by Sarah Gavitt. Reprinted by permission of the author. For performance rights, contact Smith and Kraus, Inc. (www.smithandkraus.com) E-mail: sandk@sover.net